A Practical Guide
to
Triumph Ownership

A Practical Guide
to
Triumph Ownership

The Trials and Tribulations of
Keeping Triumph TR
and Other Models on the Road

BJ Littlewood

DISCLAIMER

Should you decide to carry out any work on your vehicle based on anything written in this book you do so at your own risk. It is not a workshop manual, but a description of repairs and maintenance that the author has carried out himself and the book is only intended to preserve his experiences for other Classic Car owners. Neither the author nor the publisher will be liable for any injuries or damage caused by any person following the advice contained in this book.

The articles in this book are written by the author who is a time-served engineer, not a motor mechanic. They are based on his own practical experiences keeping his and other people's cars on the road, mainly Triumph TRs, but some other makes and models. Some are described more in depth than others as otherwise methods would be repeated.

Some articles are written in "diary" form to give a step by step /day by day guide and were written immediately after the work ended that day.

The author has owned Triumphs since 1978 and currently owns a TR4A, Herald 13/60 and a Standard Vanguard Phase 3 Vignale, all are repaired, painted, modified and serviced by the author and are used 12 months of the year to go to car shows and on runs so everything written is based on the practical experience that keeps his (and other people's) classic cars in excellent order (though not concours).

DEDICATED TO MY WIFE MICHELLE

WHOSE PATIENCE HAS ALLOWED ME TO KEEP

MY MANY CLASSIC CARS ON THE ROAD

Front cover image courtesy of my good friend Gwyn Evans.

To my Good Friend

Ray

who makes

me Smiling

Bernard

Littlewood

Contents

Section 1: Differences Between Models

How to tell Triumph TR 4, TR4A, TR 250 and TR5 models apart.

I have been asked many times about the differences between Triumph TR4 body shaped models. One person expressed their confusion at having seen two Triumph "TR4s" at a car show with one having a badge stating TR4A while the other had a badge stating TR5. Well as I am not a person who can cope with fine detail, I shall attempt to give a basic overview which will help you differentiate between the various TR4, TR4A, TR250 and TR5 models, here goes

TR4

This model was manufactured from 1961 through to 1965 and a total of 40,253 cars were made with 36,803 of these being exported (that means sent abroad Mr. Dawson). The body work was designed by Michelotti. The engine was a four-cylinder 2138cc wet liner engine and the liners can be removed to increase or decrease the cubic capacity (competition cars were sometimes reduced to 1991cc to allow them to enter "under 2000cc" category races). The engine had its origins in the Massey–Ferguson Tractor and had been modified to power Standard Vanguard models and TR2 and TR3 cars. The car also had a live rear axle. The TR4 can be visually distinguished from the other models as it does not have any chrome trim along its sides, nor does it have repeaters fitted to the front wings and the front side lights are in the grille. They were also fitted with steel wheels as standard, but many have changed these for wire or after market wheels. The bonnet badge is also the "Triumph open book" type and is central on the front of the bonnet. Some TR4s had a smaller "tear drop" bulge on the bonnet.

Triumph TR4

TR4A

This model was manufactured from 1964 to 1967 with 28,465 being made, 22,826 of these were exported. The start of production overlapped the finishing of TR4 production and I believe that although the TR4A had Independent Rear Suspension, some live axle cars were produced mainly for export to the USA. It had the same specification engine as the TR4 (I have fitted the larger 89mm bore liners to my car giving it a cubic capacity of 2290cc) and although the outer body panels remained the same there were numerous under the surface changes, the main one being the chassis for the IRS cars. They were also fitted with wire wheels as standard.

The TR4A can be visibly distinguished from the earlier TR4 by the fitted chrome side trim, the repeaters and side lights on the front wings, wire wheels (if not yet replaced by aftermarket items), and the IRS badge on the boot lid. The bonnet also has a central "Triumph Globe" badge fitted.

My TR4A, still with factory fitted standard wire wheels, note side trim and repeaters

TR5

This model had a production run from 1967 to 1968 and 2947 cars were produced. The main visual differences from the TR4A are the front grille, TR5 badges on the rear wings and boot lid and a TR5 bonnet badge positioned off set from the centre, the side chrome trims are also wider. The big difference is under the bonnet. The TR5 had a 2498cc six cylinder engine which had been developed from Triumph saloons. The engine had different compression ratios and a different camshaft along with petrol injection.

The short production run was because the TR6 was on the horizon and Triumph used the TR5 as a development stepping stone for the six cylinder fuel injected engine.

When brand new the TR5 was sometimes hard to sell as everyone knew that the new TR6 was due to be released, however, these days the rarity value of the TR5 makes it the most expensive TR to buy. It is easy to create a car with a TR5 specification, but the resale value is in having the genuine article, personally if I wanted a TR5 I would put TR6 mechanicals in my car, which I may one day carry out.

Triumph TR5

TR250

The TR250 was produced alongside the TR5 from 1967 – 1968, 8480 of these cars were manufactured and they were mainly made for the USA. Although the TR250 had the same six cylinder engine as the TR5 it was in a lower compression guise and instead of having the petrol injection system, the TR250 was fitted with twin Stromberg carburettors to enable the car to comply with USA emission tests (how times and fuel injection have changed). The cars are visually distinguishable from the TR5 by a stripe across the front of the bonnet and TR250 badges.

Triumph TR 250

GT 4R Dove

I have covered all the very basic differences within the TR4 body shape, but to confuse things a little bit more there is another variant, the GT 4R DOVE.

This car was based on the TR4 and was (I believe) developed by Standard Triumph distributors L.F. Dove of Wimbledon. There were only about 50 of these built, so if you have one, you own a very rare car.

Well I think that I have covered most bases, but as I said at the beginning, it is very much a layman's observations, although I believe that the production figures and run dates to be correct.

If any of you have any of the above cars please e mail me with any stories or issues that you have encountered and images that you have of them, perhaps I can "immortalise" them in a future book and provide encouragement to those who are contemplating taking the step into TR4, 4A,5,250 or GT 4R ownership.

I'm off for a drive in mine now because as they say "nowhere's far in a TR".

GT 4R Dove with a sunroof to give you the best of both worlds!

Section 2: Engine

Narrow Belt Conversion
(Converting the TR4A from the standard wide belt fan belt set up to a narrow belt with an electric fan installation at the same time, also addressing a timing chain issue that was found during the exercise)

The TR4A has a very wide fan belt fitted (about an inch wide) and as the radiator is a fair way away from the front of the engine there is a 4 7/8" long extension shaft for the fan which bolts onto the crankshaft pulley. To replace a broken fan belt by the roadside with this set up (although a belt of this size and strength would take some breaking!) would be an involved job as the original belt is so wide that it cannot be slipped between the radiator and fan. Another issue is that when the engine is worn (as mine was at the time) there is a tendency for the engine not to run very smoothly with the fan situated at the end of an extension shaft which is not supported and also driving such a brute of a fan belt, a combination of these factors throws the bottom end of the engine out of balance. A method of moving away from this situation is to fit an aftermarket "narrow belt conversion" which I carried out on my car in 2005, about six months after I had bought it. I also took the opportunity to convert the car to an electric fan set up at the same time. Below is an account of the exercise using notes that I had taken at the time.

After isolating the battery by removing the leads I drained the coolant and removed the radiator. I then removed the bar that braces the two front suspension turrets and gave it a good clean then sanded it down in readiness for painting with black enamel paint. Next to be removed was the fan along with its extension that bolts to the crank pulley, the dynamo, water pump pulley and crankshaft pulley were removed (using a range of pullers as they were very stubborn)in readiness for the car to be converted to the narrow type fan belt. The conversion kit that I bought did not have a new pulley for the dynamo, but as I was working at the time I had one made in the engineering workshop.

I took the radiator to a local company to have it re cored, I did not have the hole for the starter handle replicated as it would have cost a lot more money and would have been of no use as I was not going to re install the original cooling fan extension which is where the starter handle locates. I did stipulate the fitting of a thermostatic switch for use with the electric fan, but when I got the radiator home and unwrapped it, they had failed to fit one and I couldn't be bothered to take it back with the associated wait for it to be carried out. With all these parts removed I thought that I would remove the timing chain cover to replace the oil seal as it was weeping and probably had been for years. It was just as well that I did as I found that the timing chain tensioner had worn so thin that it had actually broken!

I ordered a new front oil seal, duplex timing chain and tensioner and after I had cleaned up the timing chain cover I painted it and fitted the new seal and tensioner. To replace the timing chain I first of all turned the crankshaft until the pulley key was at the bottom and the timing marks on the crank shaft chain sprockets and the cam shaft sprockets were as closely aligned as possible. The cam shaft sprocket was removed to allow the removal of the old chain and the fitting of the new chain. The crankshaft and camshaft sprockets were in amazingly good condition so I was able to re use them. The timing chain cover was then installed using a new gasket with care being taken that the tensioner was in the correct position (a trick to doing this is to use either a thin tie wrap or wire through the crankshaft hole in the cover to hold the tensioner in place, when the cover is located in position, just being held away from the block by the tie wrap, the tie wrap or wire can be withdrawn being careful not to let it damage the oil seal) before being bolted to the correct torque.

The narrow pulleys were then fitted to the crankshaft spigot, the water pump and the dynamo. The newly painted bracing bar was fitted next followed by the radiator and hoses. Next the electric fan unit was fitted to the radiator and wired up using the adjustable temperature switch and the thermo couple in the top hose (both have since been replaced by an in line thermostatic switch which is situated in the pipe that connects the bottom radiator hose to the water pump, but the adjustable one was left in situation should a problem ever occur when I'm out on a run). With the new fan belt fitted and tensioned I filled the radiator with coolant and re connected the battery.

The car started easily and the engine seemed to run a lot smoother than it had before. The broken tensioner could have been causing the valve timing to vary as well as the old steel fan on the end of an extension throwing the worn crank shaft further out of balance. When I drove the car there was a definite improvement in engine performance and smoothness, so a great result.

This set up is still in use in the car and has given good service. Since this work has been carried out I have replaced the dynamo with an alternator and rebuilt the engine. I would recommend this to any TR4/4A owner who doesn't mind moving away from originality for a likely gain in practicality.

Whether six cylinders or four, a TR is more!

TR4A Engine Rebuild October 2011

After years of running the car with its original high mileage engine I have finally decided to recondition it. I have postponed this year after year because although the engine has low compression and low oil pressure it continues to perform so well. About 5 years ago I bought a TR 4 engine and had planned to recondition this and carry out a quick swap, but as I have now retired and have more time to work on my cars I thought that I would keep the original engine. As I had planned to recondition the TR4 engine that I had purchased, I had already had the crank reground with the scroll ground away for a more modern oil seal set up and had purchased new valves, valve guides, rocker shaft, rocker arms, push rods, cam followers, camshaft, crank oil seal conversion, timing chain, pistons, rings, liners, crank bearings and camshaft bearings along with engine gaskets.

At the moment I don't know if I will remove the engine and gearbox together or just the engine, As a rule I usually remove them both together so that I can give the gear box a good internal clean, but as I installed a reconditioned overdrive gearbox 12 months ago the only benefit would be that it is easier to mate the engine and box when they are out of the car, the downside is that it would be something else that I would have to keep stepping over on the garage floor.

Although I have reconditioned many engines over the last 30 odd years I have never worked on a wet liner engine, there is a good point to a wet liner engine and a bad point. The good point is that you never need a rebore, you just replace the liners and can use different sizes to increase cubic capacity, the bad point is that if you don't get the liner height above the block correct or you don't get the lower seals to mate perfectly you will have coolant seeping into the engine oil and will have to strip the engine again. There are also conflicting views on the best figure of 8 gaskets to use (these give the seal between the seats of the block and the liners, one gasket seals 2 liners, hence the figure of 8) some are steel, some are stainless steel and some are copper, they also come in different thickness so that you can obtain the correct height that the liners must protrude above the block face so that when you torque the head down the seal is made at both ends. There is conflicting information on the height that the liners should protrude, I am opting for the +0.003" to + 0.005" dimension which is from the original TR4A workshop manual. I did install 2 of the liners into position 1 and 2 on the spare TR4 engine and the heights were +0.008" and +0.013" after using collars the thickness of the cylinder head over the head studs to torque them down, as these use the same figure of 8 gasket the only way to resolve this would be to machine 0.004" from one and 0.009" from the other, This will not pose to much of a problem if I come across the same issue with the 4A engine as a friend of mine owns a small engineering workshop and I can use one of his lathes. I will use copper figure of 8 gaskets as they will not corrode and as the head gasket is copper my opinion is that this is the best option, we'll see if I have chosen correctly when I check for coolant in the engine oil after start up!

19

11/10/2011

Today I started the engine rebuild. I drained the coolant then removed the carburettors and linkages, inlet and outlet manifolds (to do this I had to disconnect the top steering column shaft UJ and move the shaft to one side to give clearance), water pump, alternator, heater control valve, rocker cover, rocker shaft and pushrods (although I have new ones I numbered them just in case). I then loosened the head bolts and turned the engine over using the starter motor in the hope that this would help to break the cylinder head seal. It did, so I was able to remove some of the head studs to make it easier to lift the head off. Next I removed the head and then took the remaining head studs from the block.

All the studs and valves were removed from the cylinder head and the battery disconnected.

4 hours

12/10/2011

I took the cylinder head to South Wales Piston Services for hardened exhaust valve seat inserts and valve guides to be fitted, also for the head to be cleaned and if needed, skimmed.

The front of the car was raised and placed on axle stands. Next I removed the radiator and drained the engine oil.

Moving into the car's interior I removed steering wheel along with the shaft (as it was already disconnected and would give me more room), the seats, "H" section along with the CD player and controls, front carpets, gear lever and gear box cover. Next I removed the starter motor.

2.75 hours

13/10/2011

I removed the fuel pump and oil filter housing and body to engine earth strap. There was a lot of debris in the fuel pump bowl, I would have to investigate this and also fit an inline fuel filter.

I then used a wire brush attachment in my drill and cleaned up the radiator and front suspension turret brace bar.

With these cleaned up I applied 4 coats of acrylic black paint from an aerosol, but the finish is very dull (the paint might have gone off) so I would have to brush paint them when I bought new paint.

I tried to separate the inlet manifold from the exhaust manifold, but although I managed to remove the nuts, the exhaust manifold was seized to the studs, I had previously soaked these with penetrating fluid so my next move was to place the assembly in the freezer over night.

I would not be removing the engine until I return from holiday at the end of October as I would be moving the Herald outside to make room for me to work on the TR engine and I didn't want the Herald outside while I was away.

1.75 hours

14/10/2011

I removed the manifolds from the freezer and clamped the exhaust manifold in my vice then quickly applied heat from my blow torch around the studs, I gave the inlet manifold a sharp blow with a dead blow mallet and the corrosion that had held the manifold to the studs gave up its grip allowing me to separate the manifolds.

Next I gave the radiator, front brace bar and steel connecting pipe (from top of radiator to water pump) a coat of smooth Hammerite enamel.

0.75 hours

16/10/2011

I picked the cylinder head up from South Wales Piston Services and before I lapped in the valves and fit them I was going to "port" the head. To do this I bolted the two manifolds together and placed the gasket on them using the studs to ensure that they were in the correct position. This was to check that the holes in the gasket were the same size and shape as the ones in the manifolds, they were, if they had been bigger I would have had to try to source ones that were the same size or buy some blank gasket material and make new ones, if the holes had been smaller I would have had to open up the ones in the in the gasket to the exact same size and shape as the manifold ones. I then placed the gasket on the cylinder head using the locating dowels to ensure the correct position, I could see that the inlet and exhaust ports on the cylinder head were all slightly smaller than the two manifolds, this does not matter too much on the exhaust as the gasses are travelling from a smaller port into a larger pipe, however, on the inlet it is far more efficient to have the ports on the head the same size as the manifold bores so that you obtain the best flow of fuel and air. Next I scribed carefully around the gasket port holes (including the exhaust ports to eliminate any chance of "swirling" as the gasses pass into the manifold) and opened them up carefully using a small grinding stone in my Dremil. I used my automatic centre punch set to a very light punch to "dimple" the area I had ground away in the inlet ports in the head. A lot of people actually polish the ports, but I learned in my time of employment with Fuel Injection Ltd in the early 1980's that a rough finish aids the fuel/air mix and increases power and efficiency, some people will disagree with this, but I saw the before and after rolling road figures that roughening up polished inlet ports would make on the rally car engines that were prepared there.

1.5 hours

17/10/2011

I unbolted the engine to gear box studs and bolts and supported the gear box with a trolley jack and unbolted the clutch slave cylinder mounting bracket. My son Jack and I then removed the bonnet.

With the engine hoist Jack and I attempted to remove the engine leaving the gear box in position but we found that we couldn't lift the front of the engine clear of the steering rack before the gear box bell housing made contact with the bulkhead.

I replaced a few of the engine to gear box bolts, removed the angle drive for the speedo cable, undid the rear gear box to support bracket bolt and drive flange to prop shaft bolts, removed the over drive electrical connections and then lifted the engine and gear box out as one unit. It was a

very precarious operation! Probably because I have fitted a "J" type over drive unit and not the original "A" type.

3 hours

18/10/2011

The exterior of the engine was scrapped of 44 years of oil and washed down with degreaser, the gear box was new last year and did not need cleaning.

With the engine and gear box safely on the floor I unbolted the bell housing from the engine and slid the gear box away being careful to ensure that the input shaft did not touch the clutch finger springs.

Next I removed the clutch assembly and using a piece of 2" X ¼" X 3' with holes drilled to bolt to the clutch fixing holes on the fly wheel to lock it I removed the crank pulley, timing chain cover, camshaft sprocket and chain and then the flywheel.

After removing the cam followers (I am using new ones as well as a new camshaft so there is no need to number them) and withdrawing the distributor drive I undid the camshaft retaining bearing then carefully removed the camshaft. The front engine plate was then unbolted and removed. The engine was then lifted onto the engine stand and I removed the sump and oil pump. I then spent about an hour and a half degreasing and wire brushing the timing chain cover, front engine plate and lower clutch cover.

5 hours.

19/10/2011

Before stripping anything else I turned the crank until number 1 piston was at the bottom of its stroke, I then measured from the top of the piston to the top of the wet liner, this dimension of 3 5/8" will enable me to ensure that the crank that I have already had reconditioned from a spare engine and intend to fit has the same stroke.

I numbered all the con rod caps (with the numbers facing the opposite side to the camshaft) 1 – 4 with number 1 being the front of the engine then undid the bolts and withdrew them through the wet liners.

I marked the central main bearing cap with 2 centre pops on the end that faced the opposite side of the camshaft. After removing the front aluminium bridge I removed all the main bearing cap bolts and gently eased the caps out. The next to be removed was the crankshaft and then using my purpose made wet liner drift I removed the wet liners. The liner from #1 cylinder was very badly coked up.

The main bearings were still in good condition, but the big ends were in a bad way. I checked the condition of the small end bearings and remarkably they were as good as new with no sign of wear or play.

2.5 hours

20/10/2011

I fitted the new piston rings to the pistons then using new gudgeon pins and circlips assembled the pistons onto the con rods using my heat gun to warm the pistons up first so that the gudgeon pins slid in with a very slight tap.

As I have heard of problems with the tapered blind bolt that secures the clutch fork to the operating shaft shearing on other TR's I took the opportunity while the gear box was out to drill and tap a m5 hole through the centre of the fork and shaft and screwed a m5 high tensile cap head through the hole and lock it with a nyloc nut, this should prevent any problems.

Armed with the lone of Chipmunks degreaser bath and 50 litres of degreaser Jack gave the engine block and other parts a good hard brushing.

3 hours

21/10/2011

I spent 4 ½ hours cleaning the shoulders in the block where the wet liners locate of any carbon with various scrapers, then fitting the wet liners with copper figure of 8 gaskets lightly coated with Welseal and by repeatedly removing the liners and filing the 0.018" thick gaskets (you try it) I managed to obtain a consistent liner protrusion of 0.008" when the special collars that I made to hold the liners in place before cylinder head installation are torqued down.

As the recommended protrusion is 0.003" – 0.005" I had 3 choices, 1) leave it as it is and hope that when I torque the head down it makes the top and bottom seal, 2) try using the thinner steel figure of 8 gaskets (unfortunately these can corrode and don't compress to make a seal as copper does), 3) try to source thinner figure of 8 copper gaskets.

As I only had to reduce the protrusion between 0.003" and 0.005", the risk of damaging the liners if I machined them is too great.

4 ½ hours

22/10/2011

I checked on the availability of different size copper figure of 8 gaskets and the only other thicknesses are +0.005" so this takes away one option. When I filed the copper figure of 8 gaskets (holding them down on a flat surface and drawing a file over them) I found that they were no way near flat, so I therefore decided to once again remove the wet liners and use the thinner steel gaskets.

I gave the gaskets a coating of Welseal on both sides to give a better seal and to protect them from corrosion (even though they have protective plated coating) and once again fitted the wet liners. After I torqued them down using the collars there was a protrusion height of 0.004" on all liners, perfect, but I would much prefer to have used the copper gaskets. The camshaft was then installed.

1.75 hours

25/10/2011

I gave the engine block 2 coats of green(ish) engine enamel and the timing chain cover, front engine plate, lifting bracket and sump 2 coats of black engine enamel.

1.5 hours

26/10/2010

I painted the edges of the timing chain cover and sump that I hadn't been able to reach when I had previously painted them.

It was then time to install the reground crankshaft. With the engine block inverted I installed new oversize main bearings and after oiling them (some people use engine rebuild fluid or STP mixed with engine oil, the downside to this is that the protective lubricant between the bearings and crank is a couple of microns thicker, which means that when the engine is rebuilt and running this "gap" is filled by the thinner engine oil, it's down to personal choice) I carefully placed the crank in place. After inserting the standard size thrust bearings I placed a DTI on the end of the crank and checked the end float, it was 0.008". The tolerance is 0.004" to 0.006". The next size thrust bearings are +0.005", so I ordered a set from a well known supplier and if when one of the oversize bearings are fitted along with one standard one and the float is 0.003" I will reduce the oversize one by carefully rubbing if on a piece of 600 wet or dry placed on a thick piece of glass.

Next I installed the front and rear main bearing caps with new bearings ensuring that the faces were flush with the engine block.

3 hours

27/10/2011

    The oversize thrust bearings arrived and I was immediately concerned with the "made in India" sticker. I used a micrometer to measure them and although they were supposed to be +0.005", one pair was the same size as the standard bearings and one pair was +0.0055".

    I spent an hour rubbing the thicker ones with wet or dry on a piece of glass and repeatedly trial fitting them until I achieved the 0.004" end float.

I then drilled a piece of steel bar so that I could bolt it to the flywheel end of the crankshaft which would make it easier for me to rotate the crankshaft as I installed the pistons. The main bearing caps were torqued down and after scrupulously cleaning the liners and crankshaft journals the pistons and con rods were installed using my ring compressor. I temporarily used the old big end cap bolts with the intention of fitting the new bolts after checking that the engine turned over nicely with everything in place.

Another problem raised its head when I was fitting the fourth piston, the big end shell was too long and one end was protruding about 0.010" from the cap while the other end was flush, these shells had been manufactured in Israel. I very carefully filed the protrusion until it was flush with the cap, then another problem, the new big end bolts were the wrong ones, 7/16 UNF, both TR4 and TR4As use 3/8 UNF, so on the phone to  the suppliers (I will NOT buy parts from them again if they are obtainable elsewhere) and they said that they would send me the correct ones (another delay).

I soaked the felt rope in Welseal and rammed it into place in the rear main bearing cap where it seals against the recess in the block. The last action of the day was to soak the cork "T" seals with Welseal, fit them into the front aluminium bridging piece and install it so that it was flush with the front of the block, sounds easy when you write it!

All these issues with poor quality parts really impact on the time it takes to assemble an engine and the novice who may not have the equipment or background that is needed to recognise and **attempt** to rectify the faults would end up with a very poor, perhaps even scrap engine, as it is I don't know how this rebuild will turn out, as you can check the dimensions of a component, but not the quality or integrity of the material that it is manufactured from!!!!!!!!!!!!
6 hours

28/10/2011

The correct con rod big end cap bolts arrived late morning so I fitted them and torqued them down, the engine still turned over nicely. Then I realised that with all the hassle with poor quality parts I had not yet installed the rear crank oil seal (which I have converted to the newer lip seal type) so I removed the rear main bearing cap to enable this to be carried out. I then fitted the new oil pump after checking that it was within the recommended tolerances, a nice surprise, it was.

Next to be fitted was the sump using Hylomar blue on both sides of the gasket. Jack then helped me to take the engine off the stand and onto the floor using the engine hoist. The next part to be fitted was the front engine plate.

The camshaft sprocket was fitted along with the timing chain and distributor drive ensuring that the camshaft, crankshaft and distributor were all correctly timed. I used the old cam sprocket and it was an extremely tight fit on the camshaft. The next parts to be fitted were the timing chain tensioner, crankshaft oil thrower and finally the timing chain cover, I left the old oil seal in as it had been changed only a few thousand miles before along with the chain and it looked to be a better quality item than the new one that I had bought (it has two lips), should it leak I can easily change it with the engine in situ.

3.5 hours

29/10/2011

The clutch spigot bearing and flywheel were fitted and the flywheel "run out" was measured, it was 0.0025" with the limit being 0.003" so I installed the clutch friction and pressure plate using my clutch centralisation tool and torquing the bolts to the specifications in the workshop manual.

Next I offered up and mated the gear box to the engine and tightened the bolts and studs. After I fitted the flywheel inspection cover to the bottom of the gearbox bell housing I turned the engine over and there was a "grating" noise, this was caused by the cover coming into contact with the flywheel, so as I have come across this issue in the past, I overcame it by placing washers between the cover and the bell housing.

2.25 hours

30/10/2011

Our friend and fellow TSSC member Paul Price kindly offered a third pair of hands to aid the installation of the engine and gearbox, so with Jack on the engine hoist, me guiding the engine and Paul inside the car guiding the gear box we installed the engine using new engine mounts. Even with the three of us it was a precarious operation.

We then fitted the starter motor and bonnet.

2 hours

03/11/2011

The next part to be bolted back on the engine was the crank shaft pulley.

I gave the fuel pump and filter bowl a good clean out, fitted a new olive on the fuel inlet pipe and installed the pump. I then gave the oil filter housing a good clean and fitted that along with the oil pressure gauge pipe. The valves were then lapped in, first using a coarse paste and then a fine one, I only gave them a light lap as the valves were new, the exhaust seats were new and the inlet seats had been re cut.

To check if the valves were sealing I then fitted the double valve springs, retainers and collets (these I had placed on a magnet so that they became slightly magnetised and stayed in place on the valve stems while I removed the valve spring compressor, some people use grease, but as you cannot completely clean this off it can clog oil ways etc.) then with the cylinder head level, spark plugs screwed in and with the combustion chambers facing upwards I filled them with paraffin, if this did not drain away in a couple of hours I would know that the valve seats were sealing, if it drained away on any of the chambers I would have to give the valves another lapping with fine paste.

4.5 hours

04/11/2011

There had been no seepage of the paraffin overnight so the next thing to do was to clean and install all 10 cylinder head studs of which there are six different lengths, I gave the new copper head gasket a smear of Welseal on both sides and fitted the cylinder head, torquing it down to 105ftlb.

Next I dismantled the water pump and gave it a good clean, as I had installed new bearings a

few years ago I would probably re fit it even though I had a brand new spare as the old one has a grease nipple to allow periodic maintenance.

The next assembly to be stripped down was the rocker shaft, I had new rockers and a shaft which I would fit as both rockers and the shaft were badly worn.

The water pump was then cleaned with thinners and painted, the next parts that I would be reusing from the rocker assembly were wire brushed and degreased.

2.5 hours

07/11/2011

Today I assembled the rocker shaft using a new shaft and rockers. I installed it and set the valve clearances. As easy as that? No, five of the eight new rockers had to have their bushes reamed as they would not fit onto the shaft. After I had managed to locate my adjustable reamers

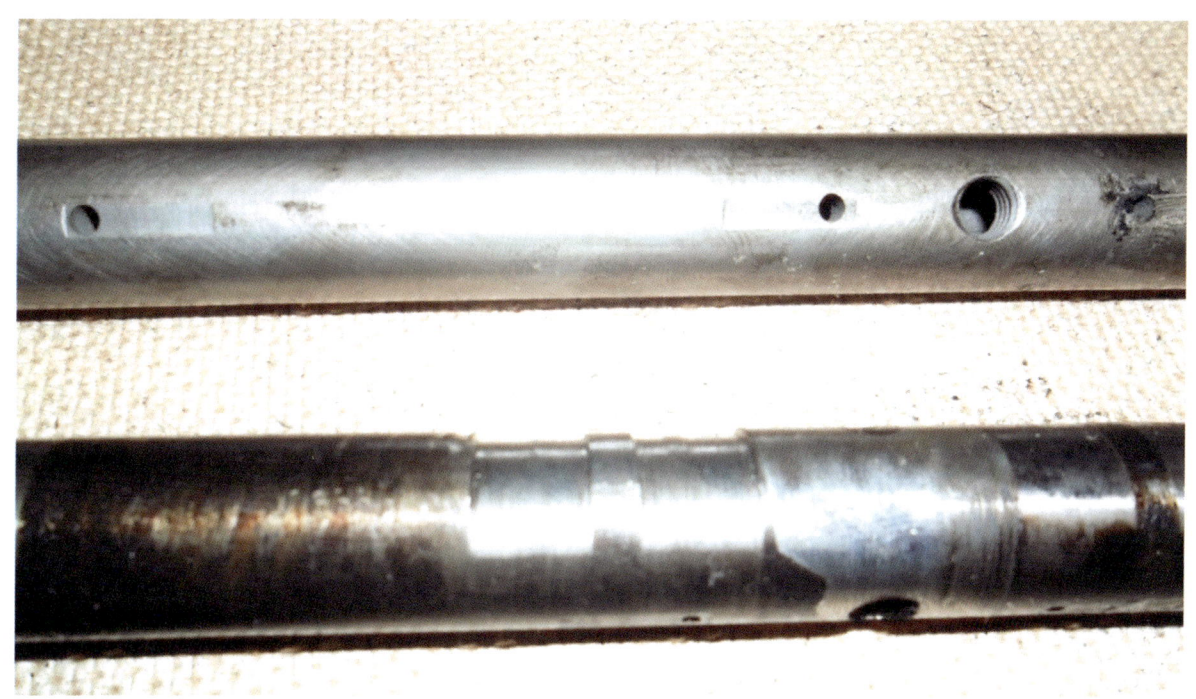

New rocker shaft at top of image, old badly-worn rocker shaft at the bottom!

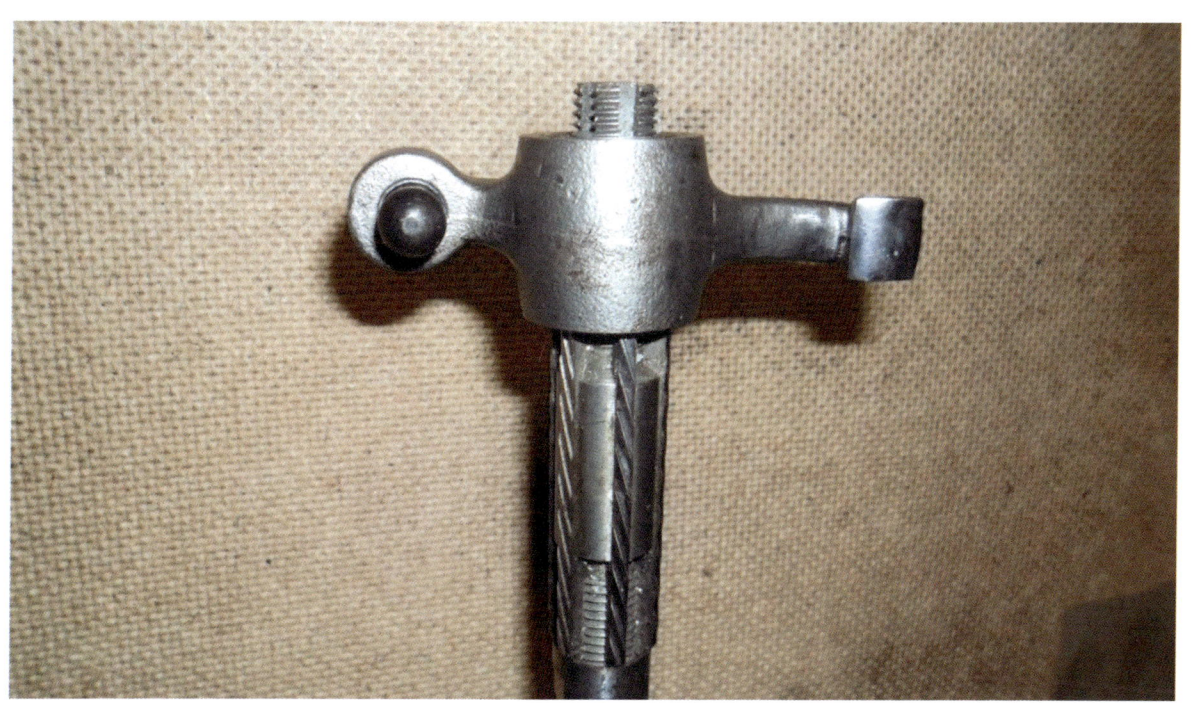

Using adjustable reamer to open up the bushes to the correct size.

Rocker shaft assembled

and find the correct one I held the reamer in my vice and adjusted it to its smallest setting, I then placed a rocker onto the reamer and adjusted the reamer until it just gripped the bush, with some lubricant I turned the rocker along the length of the reamers cutting flutes. I did this with all of the five rockers then adjusted the reamer by 1/8 of a turn and repeated the process until they were a perfect fit on the shaft, a ½ hour job now having taken 2 ½ (including the time taken to find the reamers that I had put in "a place where I wouldn't forget they" 15 years ago!) pity the person who buys these and doesn't have any reamers!

Next I installed the distributor pedestal and distributor, oil filter, rocker cover and added a few litres of engine oil.

3 hours

08/11/2011

I filled the engine up with oil, fitted the water pump and as the distributor clamp had come adrift (losing my timing marks) I removed the electronic ignition and re installed a set of points and condenser as I find it easier to set the static timing with this set up. Next I set the ignition timing and attached the rev counter cable.

A gallon of fuel was poured into the tank, and without the spark plugs in I cranked the engine over to ensure that I had oil pressure and that fuel was being pumped, there was oil pressure and the fuel was being pumped.

I fitted the inlet and exhaust manifolds, water pump pulley, fan belt and connected all the water pipes to their relative unions.

Next to be fitted were the carburettors and linkages then I connected the fuel line to the carburettors.

I had to jack up the car on its front cross member to enable me to fit the front brace that connects the two front suspension turrets. The radiator was then flushed and back flushed using a hose pipe.

All this took a fair amount of time as I cleaned up all the bolts and studs on a rotary wire brush mounted in my pedestal drill before I fitted them. I also had to touch up some of the parts with paint.

8 hours

09/11/2011

The radiator and all the hoses were fitted, then the thermostat housing and the electric fan thermocouple.

I filled the engine with 20/50 to the top mark on the dipstick and filled the radiator with a 50/50 mix of water and antifreeze and then topped up the carburettor dashpots with 3 in 1 oil.

Then with the battery connected I attempted to start the engine, after about 8 revolutions the engine fired and died. With the choke out I tried again and the engine started and ran well. I let the engine warm up then turned it off and checked the engine oil and coolant levels, they were fine. Next was the re installation of the electronic ignition and the engine was restarted. With a strobe light on number one lead I attempted to set the timing to the manufacturer's specification, but it ran more happily at about 25 BTDC, while trying a few different settings the engine started misfiring and when I pulled the leads off to find out which cylinder(s) were the cause it was 2 and 4. As I had fitted the old plugs (for running in the engine) I changed 2 and 4 for new plugs and the engine ran well. I set the timing at 20 BTDC and would keep an eye on it as I run the engine in, if it reaches the 500 mile mark with all the seals and new parts intact I can give it a good tune up then.

All I had to do now was reconnect the gearbox to the prop shaft, make all the overdrive electrical connections, install the steering wheel column and interior and give it a try, but that's another story!

2.5 hours

Engine Rebuild Footnote

Below is an account of what happened after I had completed reassembling all the remaining components and the car was ready for the road.

After taking the car for a 30-mile run, the engine was still a bit lumpy. I removed the spark plugs to find that it was running **very** rich.

I tried to adjust the jets on the carburettors but even with them adjusted right to their highest point I could not get the mixture right. I removed the dashpots and removed the needles from the pistons, I had bought the carburettors as reconditioned units a year ago and was told that they were set up for a TR4A and to be honest they proved to be excellent before I had reconditioned the engine, but as I have said the engine was badly worn.

I removed the needles and found that they had been fitted so that they had been pushed fully home into the bore in the piston, as they were the needle type with the shoulder, I re inserted them until the shoulder was flush with the piston face and locked them in position hoping that this would be enough to allow me to lower the jets and still give me a range that would allow me to adjust to the correct mixture. I then replaced the piston assemblies and dashpots and wound the jets down until they were flush with the bridge and then another 1 ¾ turns. I started the engine and it sounded much smoother so I took it for a 2 mile run then synchronised the carburettors using a Gunson balancer (I just cannot get it right by using a pipe to my ear, too many years playing drums have taken their toll). I cleaned the spark plugs and then found that I could time the ignition to around 8 degrees BTDC and then just tweak it slightly until the engine tone sounded right (it's the only way that I have ever managed to get my engines running well without pinking) I took the car for a 10 mile run, it went beautifully and when I checked the colour of all the spark plugs they were a lovely light brown.

Whether six cylinders or four, a TR is more!

TR4 Intermittent Misfire

This issue was impacting the enjoyment of using my TR, it was very frustrating trying to find and solve the problem and it took weeks to resolve even though I still used the car.

I had recently made a comment about the ongoing saga of my TR4As intermittent misfire after I had spent time checking out the ignition system: "I am confident that the misfire has been cured, chickens counted and famous last words!!"

Well didn't that come back to bite me and in a massive way as you will see if you read on. My son Jack and I travelled with seven other Triumph's to Cardigan (about 160 miles) and after about 50 miles that misfire had returned, only under 2000 rpm when pulling through the gears and only barely noticeable, but it was there! When we arrived at the show I removed number 4 and number 2 spark plugs and they were a nice colour of sandy brown. I checked the coolant level and it was still to the top of the radiator, maybe a millimetre less than before we set off, but nothing really noticeable.

After the show we set off home along the B and A roads and the misfire was there when the engine got hot, but not enough to spoil the great drive home through the Brecon Beacons. I was however, starting to think that the misfire was being caused by something more sinister than an ignition or fuel fault and although when I had reconditioned the engine I had the cylinder head pressure tested, skimmed and hardened valve inserts fitted for lead free petrol, everything was now pointing to a valve or cylinder head problem.

Here is an account of my attempts to solve the issue, the good mechanics out there that read this will no doubt both laugh and cringe at some of my methods, skills (lack of) and fault finding processes, but I am a layman and I hope that my efforts will help to give other lay people the confidence to have a go at repairing their Triumphs as I expect that there are plenty left laid up because of the cost of having the work carried out by a professional.

May 6th

The day after the show I decided that I had had enough and that I was going to go through everything to eliminate the ignition and fuel system. I cut off the spade connectors to the coil on the low tension circuit and electronic ignition circuit and soldered on new ones, I changed the plugs, leads, and distributor cap and rotor arm. I then set the carburettors going to extreme measures by setting the jet heights with a depth micrometer to ensure that they were equal, the needle protrusion from the pistons with a depth micrometer then balancing the carburettor with my carburettor balancer. After this I started the engine and it revved up cleanly so I took it for a run, it was lovely and smooth and pulled like a train with no sign of a misfire or any type of hesitancy, however, it was only when the engine was really hot (40 miles plus) that the problem was occurring so I was still sceptical that I had cured it. I thought that I would do a quick check to see the colour of the spark plug electrodes, so I removed spark plug number 4. I was very unhappy to see that when I removed the plug a very thin jet of water was coming from a hole less than the size of a pin point, this wasn't happening with the plug screwed in as the hole was on the sealing face, this must have been causing number 4 plug to get damp and to cause the misfire, it might also have been the reason that the one brand new plug fitted for the last run had broken in half when I had removed it!

I have never seen or heard anything like this before, but it meant that my cylinder head was either cracked, become porous or had suffered from internal corrosion, very disappointing after I had paid a lot of money to have this checked out before and I'm not at all happy. I checked prices of reconditioned cylinder heads and they were between £1500 and £1800 plus carriage and in most cases a surcharge until the old head (which had to be serviceable) was received.

I resisted the urge to remove the cylinder head straight away, I had a bit of thinking (drinking) to do as I had a 6 cylinder Triumph 2000 TC engine in my shed and I was tempted to check out the main and big end shells and if serviceable, drop the engine in my TR, at least the 6 cylinder engine has affordable and available spares and I would get my TR4A or would that be TR2000TC on the road in the near future. Even if I had just removed the cylinder head and replaced it with a new one (or perhaps find someone who can repair mine) there was a danger that the wet liners would become unseated from the figure of 8 seals, so it looked like I'd be using my 13/60 convertible for the next few shows and road runs, although with the Pencoed Show only 6 days and 30 odd miles away I could have used the TR for that and then again for the Vale of Glamorgan show. I thought that I would try to insulate the spark plug and temporarily plug the water leak by coating the spark plug threads and sealing washer with Wellseal. I wasn't happy I wouldn't get far in my TR!

May 7th

After sleeping on my decision to carry on using the TR I did my usual U turn and decided to remove the cylinder head. So after first draining the coolant then removing the carburettors, inlet manifold and exhaust manifold (disconnecting the steering column shaft to allow room to remove the manifolds) I turned my attention to removing the water pump (only to allow me a bit more room to work) the rocker cover and the rocker shaft. With the spark plugs removed all that was left to do was to try to take the head off without unseating the wet liners! With two wooden hammer handles in the furthermost ports I levered gently and felt the seal between the head/gasket/block break. I tried pulling the head off, but to no avail. I locked two nuts together on each head stud and removed the 10 cylinder head studs (as they had only been in place 18 months I did not have too much trouble doing this). With the studs removed I lifted the head off and in the hope that the wet liners had not moved I locked them in position with the spacers that I had had made before the engine rebuild in 2011. The head was taken to a local engine specialist for assessment, the person who served me asked if I "just wanted to chance them fitting an insert into the plug area and refitting the head" I managed to stay polite and said that I wanted it pressure tested and if a repair was a possibility I wanted it carried out and then pressure tested afterwards, nothing less than a first class job was acceptable, no matter what the cost (after all it was going to be a lot less than £1800, wasn't it?). They said that they would call me the next day.

While waiting for the call I spent hours on the internet looking for the best way to proceed should the expected bad news materialise and sent numerous e mails to various parts suppliers and engine rebuild specialists.

It took me 2 ½ hours to remove the cylinder head from my car.

May 8th

After repeated phone calls to the engine specialists, late in the afternoon I eventually received the expected bad news, "your head is not repairable, that will be £43.70 please!"

So back onto the internet and after a lot of haggling I managed to source a complete and refurbished cylinder head from Germany for around £1500 + surcharge as they wanted my old head no matter what its condition was. They had a site 172 miles away from my home (I would have preferred to pick the new head up when I dropped my old one off, but for some reason they couldn't accommodate this) and I managed to make a deal that would see the cylinder head delivered to my house directly from Germany and I would not have to pay the surcharge if I delivered my old head to the address 172 miles away (probably cheaper than sending it by courier due to its weight and a lot less hassle than sending it), unfortunately by the next day for some reason the cost had risen to £1900!

May 9th

I picked up my broken cylinder head from the engine repair specialist and returned home to find two welcome e mails. The first was an offer from an Engineering Company of a reconditioned cylinder head with unleaded conversion complete with valves for £1350 including vat and delivery and for this price my head was not required.

The second was the offer from a TR specialist of a brand new old stock cylinder head that had been converted to lead free and also complete with valves for £1530 including vat and delivery, this was also a straight purchase without a re conditional head required in part exchange.

I had a good think and in the end I decided to opt for the new head, only because I don't expect to ever get the opportunity to buy an original new head ever again. I made the phone call and the deal was struck with next day delivery a real possibility.

May 10th

The cylinder head arrived early in the afternoon and after cleaning the protective coating off it I started the re assembly process. I noticed that the new head didn't have the manifold location dowels and no matter what I tried including warming the old head and also using a "freezing" spray on the dowels, I could not remove them without damaging them. I did think of cutting up the shank of a 5/16" drill, but as I was taking the 13/60 to the Pencoed show two days later I was in no real hurry and besides after spending the amount I had on the new head I wanted the job to be as good as I could make it, so I made a phone call and asked for as fast a delivery as possible for the two dowels plus a few other items. Next I removed the spacers that were keeping the wet

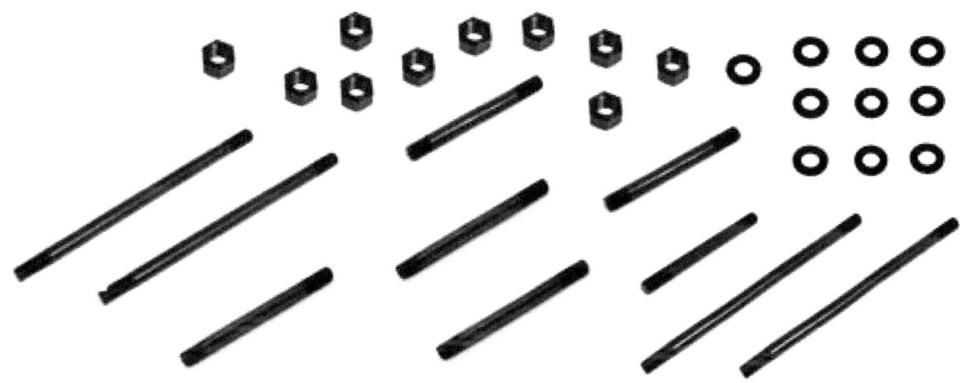

liners in place, coated the engine block face with Wellseal, slid the head gasket onto the few head studs that I had put in position to ensure that the gasket lined up then coated the head gasket with Wellseal and slid the head into position. Next I had to sort out the remaining head studs, There are 10 studs and 5 different lengths, 3 are 5" long, 1 is 5 9/16" long, 2 are 5 3/8" long, 2 are 9" long and 2 are 9 ½" long, so it's easy to get the 5 9/16" mixed up with the 5 3/8" ones. With the head studs locked in place I fitted the cylinder head and torqued the head nuts to 102 foot pounds working gradually up and starting from the middle nuts as directed in the workshop manual. The next parts to be re installed were the pushrods and rocker shaft, The valve clearances were then set to 0.010" (another operation that is made easier with the water pump removed as I could easily get a spanner on the crankshaft nut to turn the engine over, I have an electric fan so there is no mechanical fan with the extension on my car). This took me 3 hours.

May 11th

With an early start I managed to re install the water pump, rocker cover, breather valve, heater valve, water hoses and fill the radiator up with coolant using a 50/50 water to antifreeze mix. This sounds like it was quick and easy, but with having to clean old gaskets and sealant off (yes I should have done that on the 9th!) it took me a few hours as I'm not the tidiest of workers and a lot of that time was spent looking for the correct fittings, although in my defence there was one very tired looking exhaust stud and although I had a selection of spare studs they were all ¼" and I needed 5/16" and so I had to cut up a long 5/16" UNF bolt that was only partially threaded and cut a m8 thread on the other end as I couldn't find my 5/16" UNC (or UNF) die, rooting around for these took me an hour. I also took the opportunity to dismantle and maintain all the ball and socket joints on the carburettor linkages (a separate article). Then right on cue the postman arrived with my dowels, so after fitting them I cleaned the old gaskets off my exhaust and exhaust manifold and fitted it using new gaskets and exhaust sealant on the manifold to exhaust gasket. Next on was the inlet manifold closely followed by the carburettors and linkages. It was then that I realised that I could not reconnect the steering shaft as it was now the "wrong side" of the carburettors, so I had to remove the shaft from its bottom coupling to get it back in place. With that done, I fitted the spark plugs and crossed my fingers. The engine started on the third turn and revved up well.

I took the car for a 12 mile test run and after 5 miles it was "missing like a pig" and suffering from bad pre ignition. So back on my drive I set the ignition timing statically at TDC then adjusted it with the engine running until it sounded "happier". I then checked the colour of the spark plugs and the mixture was very weak, so I enriched the mixture after which I re balanced the carburettors. With this done I took the car for another blast up the M4 from junction 30 to 32 (a round trip of about 12 miles) and the car went well, but there was slight pre ignition when I turned the engine off.

I checked the dipstick to see if any coolant had contaminated the engine oil (this would mean the figure of 8 gaskets had been disturbed) and it seemed fine. The level of coolant in the radiator had fallen, but hopefully only because of an air lock when I initially filled it.

I wanted to take the car on the Carmarthenshire road run the following weekend so I hoped that I would be able to get some miles on the clock during the week to settle in the new head and then re tune the timing and carburettors.

Please note: by Pre ignition (my layman's definition) I mean that the engine "runs on" after the ignition is switched off or if I am under the bonnet, the feed to the coil pulled off.

This work took 5 ½ hours.

MAY 13th

After a great day out at Pencoed classic car show in my 13/60 convertible, I totally ignored my own advice and turned my attention to tuning the TR in readiness for the Carmarthenshire road run.

I thought that I would double check everything, so to start off I checked the valve clearances and two seemed to have closed up by about 0.002" (head gasket settling in? Beats me). So I started the engine and let it warm up, with it nice and hot I checked the timing statically, then adjusted it until the engine felt happiest although it was revving high and there was no adjustment left on the carburettors. To get around this, I removed the dashpots and pistons (please note that on some SU carb dashpots you need to mark their positions as they have to go back in the same place, on my carbs the fixing holes are positioned so that they can only be fitted one way) and lowered both the needles (checking with my depth micrometer – overkill?) in the hope that I would obtain more adjustment, thankfully I did. Then with the jets reset to 2 turns down from being level with the bridge (and checked with my depth micrometer) I used my carburettor balancer to tune the carburettors (again) and then checked the ignition timing with my stroboscope for reference, it was 20 degrees BTDC. I took the car on my 12 mile test route and it ran very well apart from the smell of petrol which was coming from the float bowl of the front carburettor and some pre ignition if I revved the engine and turned it off. I had new floats and valves and gaskets which I fitted, but nothing I did would stop the (now intermittent) leak!!! Why did all these other faults occur when they were not there before!

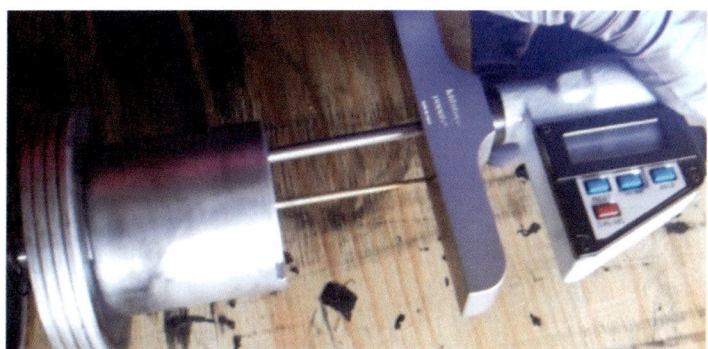 

I made a phone call to Burlen and ordered a pair of their VITON RUBBER tipped float valves in the hope that they would make a better seal than the standard brass ones (I had installed the type that used a ball valve years ago and they leaked continuously, however, technology has moved on and I know of people who are very pleased with the ball type valve) and hoped they would arrive in time for me to fit them before the Carmarthenshire road run, but if the float valves were not the problem then the only thing that I could think of is could the pressure of the fuel delivery be too high (but it wasn't an issue before I changed the head), so with this in my mind I jumped on my PC and ordered a fuel pressure regulator. Returning to the car I retarded the ignition timing and then took it for another test run. All seemed to be fine and the fuel leak did not rear its head, however, I hoped that the fuel pressure regulator would arrive in time for me to fit it before the big test, the Carmarthenshire road run in 6 days' time.

A point to note is that I do not recommend the settings that I use as being correct for all TR4As, these are the settings that my car runs better at, I always use the manufacturers base settings then tweak them to suit my car, I'm not saying that this is the right thing to do, but it works for me and after all if all car engines and ancillaries were set to the manufacturer's settings there would be no work for engine tuners.

This took 4 hours!!

May 15th

I decided to take the car along my usual 12 mile test run on the M4, it started well and ran well with no sign of the fuel leak, but when I revved the engine and turned off the ignition there was pre ignition, I adjusted the timing until the pre ignition disappeared and now the engine revs were higher and I had run out of adjustment on the carburettors. I have never been happy with the carburettors, I bought them as reconditioned a few years ago and the jets had

sometimes stuck in the down position when I have used the choke, so as I had ordered new float valves I decided that I should buy new needles and jets and fit them in the hope that I would be able to set the engine up so that I had ample adjustment.

With this in mind I ordered new jets and needles then I removed and stripped both carburettors and checked them out. The throttle discs were perfectly aligned and there was no play at all in the throttle spindles, however, the lug on the body of the front carburettor that keeps the float chamber in position was missing (obviously sheared off in the past and not replaced when the carburettor was reconditioned). I removed the jets and even though I had new ones on order I rubbed them down with fine wet or dry paper until they were a nice sliding fit in the jet bodies, just in case the new ones didn't arrive in time for me to fit them before the Carmarthenshire run on 19th.

It took about 1 ½ hours to carry this out.

May 16th

Well the needles and jets hadn't arrived yet so I re assembled the carburettors, to centralise the jets, with the pistons (complete with needles set with the shoulder level with the piston face), springs and dashpots installed I used a pencil to push the piston down (through the damper hole) and tightened the jet locking nut then ensured that the pistons operated freely and made the nice "metallic click" as they fell on to the bridge. I fitted the springs and jet adjusting nuts along with the jets and set them 2 turns below the top of the bridge. Using new seals for the jet feeding pipe to float bowl connection I gave the nuts a good "nip up". With the choke linkages fitted I checked the operation of the jets and they returned perfectly when I put the linkages in the off position. I then installed the carburettors complete with linkages.

As there had been pre ignition no matter where I had set the timing I decided to fit my spare distributor with its points set up to eliminate any electronic ignition/distributor fault and I set it statically with the mark on the crank pulley lined up with the pointer on the timing chain cover on the firing stroke of number one cylinder.

I started the car and tuned in the carburettors and although the car ran well on my 12 mile test run there was still slight pre ignition. When the carburettors were dismantled I had taken measurements of the needles so that I could measure the new ones when they arrived and try fitting them if there was a difference.

Another issue also reared its ugly head, there was an unhealthy noise from the starter motor/flywheel when starting the car, there was a high torque starter motor on my car and I could only reach the top fixing nut by removing the gear box cover inside the car, I didn't have the time to take it out and inspect the flywheel and starter so I crossed my fingers that it would last until after the Carmarthenshire road run!

Another 4 hours spent doing this.

May 17th

Well that ugly noise was even worse when I started the car to take it for a run so I had to investigate. I removed the "H" section that supports the dashboard along with all the switches and CD player then removed the carpets and gearbox cover. Next I removed the starter motor and could see that the flywheel ring gear was showing signs of slight damage on the engine side, but it wasn't too bad, I attached the starter to a spare battery and it was shot! Luckily I had kept the original starter motor so when I eventually found it I gave it a quick service and tested it, it seemed fine so I installed it (disconnecting the steering shaft to gain enough room to ease the physically larger motor into position). As I had misplaced the original starter motor bolts I had to cut down two longer bolts and cut threads on them long enough to accommodate the starter and spacer, but with this done I finally fitted it and turned the ignition key, the engine turned over and started. I left it at that knowing that I had one more day to try to get the TR driveable for the Carmarthenshire run.

This took me 4 ½ hours

May 18th

Not being able to sleep I found myself in my garage at 3am to start quietly re installing the car's interior, before I installed the gear box cover I made a cut out in it and a cover held in place with self tapping screws after I had marked out the position where the top starter motor bolt could be accessed so that I would be able to easily remove the starter motor without removing the gear box cover and everything else that would entail this in the future.

With everything back in place and the time being 8:30am I attempted to start the car and guess what, it started! I took it for my 12 mile test run and the car went well, but there was bad pre ignition and I couldn't set a decent tick over as I had run out of adjustment on the carbs. I removed the carbs and as the new parts had now arrived I installed the new needles (0.015" longer than the original ones) and jets along with the float valves. With these fitted I was able to obtain a nice tick over, but there was still a bit of pre ignition after a test run. I tried retarding and advancing the ignition timing, but nothing I did made a difference. I checked the spark plugs and they showed a weak mixture, so I lowered the jets another 1/3 of a turn. That was all I could do and I intended to take the car on the Carmarthenshire run the next day and check the plugs at various stops and adjust the mixture accordingly. I also decided to source some spark plugs that would allow the engine to run cooler. If none of this worked I would have to start thinking that the cylinder head is the problem in some way.

The longest part of this job was re installing the interior parts, in all it took 7 ½ hours.

MAY 19th - Day of the Carmarthenshire Road Run

My son Jack and I set off in the TR at 7am, the car started first time, so we set off westwards along the M4 to the first rendezvous point. Then a tapping noise started from under the bonnet at about 2000rpm, "I'm not stopping on the hard shoulder" I thought, it's only about 20 miles to the rendezvous, I also realised that I hadn't checked the to see if the horn was working after the steering shaft had been disturbed, I checked, it wasn't.

We arrived at the rendezvous point where we were meeting other Triumph owners and I opened the bonnet and found that a spare earth lead that I carry in case I lose the red cut off key had become un clipped leaving it free to knock against the battery box, could this have been the cause of the tapping? I slackened the two bolts in the block clamp that allow the steering shaft to slide and pushed it down about 1/16" which allowed the horn pencil to make contact and operate

43

the horn (I have a non standard steering wheel and if I have the shaft fully down the boss makes earth to the steering column top on hard cornering which causes the horn to operate). Then I checked the spark plugs, they showed the engine to be running very weak so I lowered the jets 1/3 of a turn each and adjusted the tick over.

We then left for the next rendezvous again westwards along the M4, no tapping, just the TR running better than it ever has and after the 50 mile mark was passed there was no sign of any petrol smell or a misfire! At the next rendezvous I checked the plugs and again I enriched the mixture by 1/3 turn on each jet, the car was ticking over nicely, but still had pre ignition no matter how I "tweaked" the ignition timing. We covered 286 miles that day with the roof off in glorious sunshine and the car returned 31mpg, but it was still appearing to be running weak and had pre ignition. I now suspected that air is being drawn in somewhere although spraying all joints with WD40 revealed no change in the engine note, I would have to investigate further.

May 21st

Monday 20th I ordered two sets of cooler type spark plugs (1 set a grade cooler and 1 set 2 grades cooler) and a set of needles for the carburettors that should give me a richer mixture. I borrowed a friend's pressure drop testing kit and with each piston TDC on their firing strokes no air loss through the valves (or anywhere else) was indicated. Although I would have to remove the cylinder head if I wanted to check the volume of the combustion chambers (lesson well learnt, I will never fit a new head without doing this first in the future) I decided to check the thickness of the new head against the old one. Using my depth micrometer and allowing (as far as was possible) for the head gasket, the new head was about 0.012" thicker which would indicate that the "light skim to remove surface rust" information from the supplier on the new head was correct and that the head had not had been over skimmed. I removed the carburettors and manifolds and checked the indentation on the gaskets which indicated a good seal had been made, however, when I placed the inlet manifold onto the new head without a gasket (holding it lightly in place with the clamps) I could insert a 0.006" feeler gauge between the centre of each flange. With this straw firmly grasped I used a straight edge and using my past skills of draw filing from my apprenticeship days (they told me it would come in handy one day) I carefully removed the high spots after spraying the flanges with black paint between each "filing" to show me where the metal had been removed. When I was satisfied that the faces were as flat as I could reasonably hope to achieve I re assembled the manifolds and carburettors with new gaskets. The engine was started and after tuning the carbs I was able to tweak the ignition timing until the engine stopped with only the faintest pre ignition if I revved the engine and turned the ignition off, but hopefully this was just because the engine was now very hot. I decided to leave it at that and to test drive the car the next day, and I also had the option of fitting the cooler type plugs and "richer" needles.

Another 5 hours spent doing this work.

May 22nd

The car started easily with choke so I took it for a test drive and it performed faultlessly, when I turned the ignition off there was slight pre ignition, but instead of leaving well alone, I removed the distributor as I noticed that it felt a bit "notchy" when I had previously slackened the clamp (and the anchoring nuts to enable the clamp to release) and found that the area where the clamp located on the body was crumbling away. I ordered a new distributor through a well known auction site with the view to either re fitting my electronic ignition into the new distributor or using the main body (if it was compatible) with the original internal parts from my old distributor (I had previous bad experiences with pattern distributors) to ensure that I retained the correct advance and retard specifications. And to continue my current run of luck I then found 2 x 25D distributors that I had previously bought as spares! They were from an unknown model of car so the internal parts from my original distributor still had to be used. I wanted to get some more miles on the clock first and there was a show coming up in the Vale of Glamorgan on the 27th (only a 38 mile round trip) and the Pembrokeshire show on June 2nd which would be roughly a 220 mile round trip, after these I could re torque the head and try a bit more fine tuning. I re fitted the distributor and could not find the timing point where there was only slight pre ignition, so I fitted the 1 grade cooler type spark plugs, they made no difference!

Just an hour spent today.

May 23rd

I removed the distributor and stripped it down to its component parts and after doing the same to one of my spare distributors I fitted the TR4A specification shaft and bob weight assembly. With this installed I could still not get rid of the pre ignition so I made a phone call to a well known engine specialist (a big thank you to the chap who spent most of his lunchtime talking to me, making sure that I had covered everything, unfortunately I had) and their advice was to open up the valve clearances to 0.012". As I was about to go out on a run in my 13/60 I called it a day and to be honest I didn't think the advice would help.

Again just an hour spent today

May 24th

I removed the rocker cover and started to open up the valve clearances to 0.012" but when I came to adjust number 1 cylinder exhaust valve I could not get it to go any bigger than 0.010"! On close inspection I found that the shoulder at the top of the pushrod was coming into contact with the tappet (rocker arm) at exactly 0.010". Could the pushrod be expanding enough when hot to close up the clearance as it was not able to pivot in its ball and socket connection to the rocker arm and cause the pre ignition? Was this happening on any other valve? I didn't check I just knew I had to eradicate this issue. I made up some 0.032" aluminium shims (with an oil feed hole for the one) and placed them under the rocker shaft pedestals then set the valve clearances to 0.012".

When I started the car and let it get hot NO PRE IGNITION! I took the car for a run, NO PRE IGNITION, NO MISFIRE!

I returned home and reset the carburettors and the ignition timing to the recommended settings then fine tuned them. I took the car for another run and it ran beautifully (although sounding tappety). There was no misfire and no pre ignition when I turned the ignition off. I was not going to count my chickens again yet, but I now intended to take it as it was to the Pembrokeshire Classic Car show on 02/06/2013 and maybe (if my wife and daughter didn't want to come) to the Vale of Glamorgan Show on 27th May.

Another four hours spent working on the car today.

May 27th

Well my wife and daughter decided that they did not want to go to the Vale of Glamorgan show as the weather forecast was bad for the afternoon, so my son Jack and I went in the TR. It was only a 19 mile journey, but when we arrived and I turned the engine off, there was very slight pre ignition! I retarded the timing slightly and after checking the spark plugs I enriched the mixture by 1/3 of a turn on each carburettor. On the return journey there was heavy traffic so I took the opportunity when the traffic wasn't moving to turn the engine off, there was pre ignition so I pulled into a lay by and advanced the timing very slightly, the car ran well after this and there was no pre ignition, but with the Pembroke Classic car show in six days time I knew I would have to investigate further still! I wasn't happy.

May 28ᵗʰ

I started the car and when it reached operating temperature there was very slight pre ignition when I revved the engine before turning off the ignition, but not anywhere as bad as before I had shimmed the rocker pedestals. I dismantled the new distributor that I bought (as I had to cut down the post that the advance and retard spring located on to fit the electronic ignition sensor) and installed my luminition electronic ignition. With the timing set to 8 degrees BTDC at 800rpm there was very slight intermittent (sometimes it would occur, sometimes it wouldn't) pre ignition, so I installed a set of spark plugs that were two grades cooler than the standard type. I also installed the needles that I had bought that should enrich the mixture as the spark plugs showed that the mixture was a bit weak. I then once more checked that the carburettors were balanced. With these settings the engine only ran on only very slightly when I revved the engine then turned it off. After each change of settings I took the car for a test run. I removed the rocker cover and spark plugs and even though the engine was hot none of the valve clearances seemed to have closed up. I decided to re torque the head and set the valve clearances (to 0.010") the next day when the engine was cold, if the pre ignition only occurs when I rev the engine then turn it off I will have to learn to live with it or find another cylinder head to try, there is no way that the settings of the timing and carburettors should be so sensitive!

All this took my 5 hours and probably 2 gallons of petrol!

May 29ᵗʰ

With the engine cold, I removed the rocker cover, it's fixing studs, the heater valve (after draining some coolant) and spark plugs. Next the head was torque down and I set the valve clearances to the manufacturer recommended gap of 0.010". With everything back in place I took the car for a run and there was no sign of any pre ignition. My intention was to leave it like that and see how the car performed on the Pembrokeshire Classic Car show run (a round trip of just over 200 miles) in four days time.

About an hour spent on this.

June 2ⁿᵈ

Well I managed to keep my hands off the TR for a few days and on the morning of the Pembrokeshire show the TR started first time with plenty of choke. Jack and I enjoyed a great 109 mile drive with the TR performing faultlessly to the show and there was no sign of the engine running on (what I am referring to as pre ignition) at the various rendezvous points. When the engine had cooled down I removed spark plugs 1 and 4 to find that they were very sooty so I raised each jet ½ a turn. I had expected that the fuel consumption would have been very high because of the plug colour so at the start of our return journey I filled the tank up and the car had been returning 32mpg! We had a stop for a natural break and I checked the spark plugs 1 and 4 and this time they were a nice brown colour. So, with a 223 mile round trip (including a detour for fuel) I felt I had cause for cautious optimism. The only glitch that day was the original bonnet release cable jamming the latch open which meant the bonnet popped up a few times until I disconnected the cable and relied on the reserve cable and emergency latch opening device to release the latch until I sorted out the original one. When I arrived home I checked the spark plugs

1 and 4 and they were once more a bit black and sooty so I changed the spark plugs for the 1 grade cooler ones.

June 9th

Well (apart from fitting a new bonnet release cable) I managed to keep my fingers from tampering with the TR for a whole week! I took the car to the Barry Festival of transport and after a fantastic day in sun with the TR performing faultlessly I decided to check the spark plugs when I returned home (even though Barry is only about 21 miles from my house) and the plugs were black and sooty, however, as I was due to take the TR on the Under Milk Wood run the following Saturday with a camp over on the Saturday night on the Gower Coast followed by the Swansea Festival of Transport on the Sunday I decided not to make any alterations to the TR as there had been no sign of any pre ignition. So first thing the next morning I changed the needles in the carburettors for the standard ones that I had changed for the "richer mixture" ones that were in the car!

June 11th

After an invitation to visit the Wyedean (a 90 mile round trip) I checked the spark plugs to find that they were still a bit black so I weakened the mixture by ½ a turn on each jet.

Have I finally resolved the issue?

June 15th – Under Milk Wood run

Jack and I set out in the TR for the Under Milk Wood run, starting at Bracelet Bay Swansea and finishing at Dylan Thomas's Boat House. The TR performed faultlessly with no misfire or pre ignition. We were camping for the night on the Gower coast and attending the Swansea Festival of Transport the next day so I filled the tank up a few miles before we arrived at the Gower and after 142 miles of varied driving (very heavy traffic at the start of the run) the TR was returning 32mpg!

When our camp was set up I checked the spark plug colours and they were indicating a slightly weak mixture (at least this showed me I was very close to the best settings as every other time they had been showing a rich mixture) so I turned the jets down one flat on the adjusting nut.

June 16th

The TR started first time and again performed faultlessly on the run to Swansea and then home after the show. On returning home I checked the colour of the spark plugs and they still indicated a slightly weak mixture so I thought I would fit the standard spark plugs and see if that helped, but I was 99.99% there, and I think most people would leave the settings as they are at this point. I had even been encouraged by my friend John turning up to travel with us to the Swansea show in his immaculate TR3, as when he turns his engine off even with no revs, it runs on and he has an anti run on valve fitted.

Conclusion

Well, I know that the fuel these days can cause issues with an old Triumph and can give ignition problems, but my TR had not suffered with any that I could not alter ignition and carburettor settings to eradicate before the new cylinder head issue so let's look back on how I finally resolved the issue.

1) The issue with the push rod fouling the rocker arm at spot on 0.010" valve clearance and perhaps closing up the clearance when hot was solved by shimming the rocker pedestals. I believe that this was the main issue.

2) Although there was no change in engine note when I sprayed WD40 on the inlet manifold joint, there was a 0.006" gap when the manifold was placed against the head without a gasket, this was solved by filing the face of the manifold until it was flat.
3) New Burlen needles and jets were fitted along with the rubber type float valves to eradicate any over fuelling (I bought a fuel pressure regulator, but although I installed it under the bonnet, I have not as yet plumbed it in).

A lesson learnt – I will never fit a different cylinder head without first of all checking the volume of the combustion chambers or checking the overall thickness of the cylinder head even when it is new as the one I bought was and not a reconditioned one, it's too late to do this when installed! If the engine was not a wet liner type I would have removed the cylinder head immediately to check it, but the risk of disturbing the figure of eight seals was too great. There were many times during this exercise that I felt *very* frustrated and close to fitting the 6 cylinder engine that I have for future use in one of my cars, but as soon as that TR engine fires up and I'm on either a fast open road or meandering around country lanes it makes every second spent working on the car worthwhile.

It is now January 2019 and the TR has performed faultlessly, averaging 31 mpg and with no sign of a miss fire or pre ignition.

A Simple Tip When Removing a Canister-type Oil Filter:

Over the years I have been asked a few times about the best way to remove "stubborn" oil filters (the canister spin off type). I have the more modern spin off filter conversion on my 4A and yes, it is very close to the engine block, I have a strap type filter wrench and although I can get it around the filter I would have to remove the fuel pump to gain enough purchase on the wrench's handle. Here is how I remove my filter if it won't turn unscrew by hand; I put a jubilee clip (you can join a few together if you don't have one large enough) around the filter, tighten it up and then with a long punch on the scroll/screw part of the clip, I tap the punch to loosen the filter off, I can then usually undo the jubilee clip and remove the filter by hand, if not I keep repositioning the clip and tapping it so that I can gradually slacken off the filter until it comes off by hand. Another method is to hammer an old screwdriver into the side of the filter and turn the screwdriver to slacken off the filter, the problem with this method is that not only is it messy, but if you position the screwdriver wrongly you could damage the thread that the filter screws on to, you would also probably end up having to make a few holes as there is not enough room to turn the filter very far with a screwdriver in it. If, on a TR4A for example, you end up having to remove the filter conversion housing you will need to replace the O ring, but to keep it in place when re fitting the housing, smear the O ring with petroleum jelly (Vaseline).

How to Change a Valve Spring, Valve Stem Oil Seal, or Ease a Sticking Valve Without Removing the Cylinder Head:

A friend of mine who carries out his own maintenance on his TR6 and had just had the cylinder head off to have it converted to use lead free petrol along with all new valves and valve guides told me that he had to remove the head again as one of the valves was sticking now and again, he had noticed that it had been a bit tight on assembly but thought that it would "run itself in" after a few miles, I gave him the following advice which solved the problem, this method can also be used to change valve springs and/or valve stem seals.

Remove the rocker cover, spark plugs and rocker shaft, turn the engine over until the piston in the cylinder with the sticking valve is at its lowest point (thin screwdriver or similar down the spark plug hole to feel it), then push a very long length of nylon string down into the cylinder through the spark plug hole until you can get no more in leaving a length protruding from the spark plug hole. Turn the engine over clockwise (by hand, disconnect battery) until the engine "locks" which means that the piston has jammed the nylon string against the valves. Remove the collets and springs from the sticking valve (it can't fall in as it is held by the compressed nylon string), turn the engine over anticlockwise so that the valve is no longer jammed against the string and using a pistol/cordless drill, hold the valve stem in the drill's chuck and using a thin oil to lubricate the valve guide, rotate the valve anti clockwise and clockwise alternatively until the valve stem "runs itself in" and is a nice fit in the guide. When it is, rotate the engine clockwise, until the valve is fully closed against the nylon string, replace the springs, collets, turn the engine anticlockwise and pull the string out then fit the rocker shaft and set your valve clearances.

I had a phone call from him the following day saying that he had acted on my advice and that the car was now running perfectly. He had saved the cost of a new head gasket and anti freeze as well as quite a few hours of his time.

GT6 Cylinder Engine Head Refurbishment
Although this work was carried out on a GT6, the same process would be used for a TR250 (also TR6 and TR5 for the actual head work).

One of the S. Wales TSSC club members had been struggling with the performance of his GT6 for a few years, the engine had been replaced by a reputable Triumph dealer with a "reconditioned" unit (the engine number denoted it as a Triumph 2000 Mk2) and since the engine had been installed the car had covered 15,000 miles. Over many club (and other) runs the car had suffered "ignition and carburetion" issues which the owner had attempted to address by fitting new top quality parts (after all the engine was a reconditioned unit wasn't it? Can't be an engine issue!), but to no avail. He finally lost patience when a "miss fire" was traced to an inlet rocker separating itself from its pushrod and as his time was at a premium he asked me to have a look at it, here is the tale of my "investigations".

The first thing that I checked was the compression, the results being -
Cyl 1 = 90 PSI
Cyl 2 = 100 PSI
Cyl 3 = 105 PSI
Cyl 4 = 84 PSI
Cyl 5 = 81 PSI
Cyl 6 = 106 PSI

Not good at all and as the results hardly changed with the addition of oil into the bores and testing again there was only one thing for it, the head had to be removed.

After unbolting the exhaust from the manifold I disconnected the choke and throttle cable then removed the manifold nuts, the manifolds (inlet complete with carbs) came away without trouble. The heater valve, water pump and thermostat housing were then removed after a lot of persuasion as the bolts in the thermostat housing were seized solid. After the rocker cover was removed I

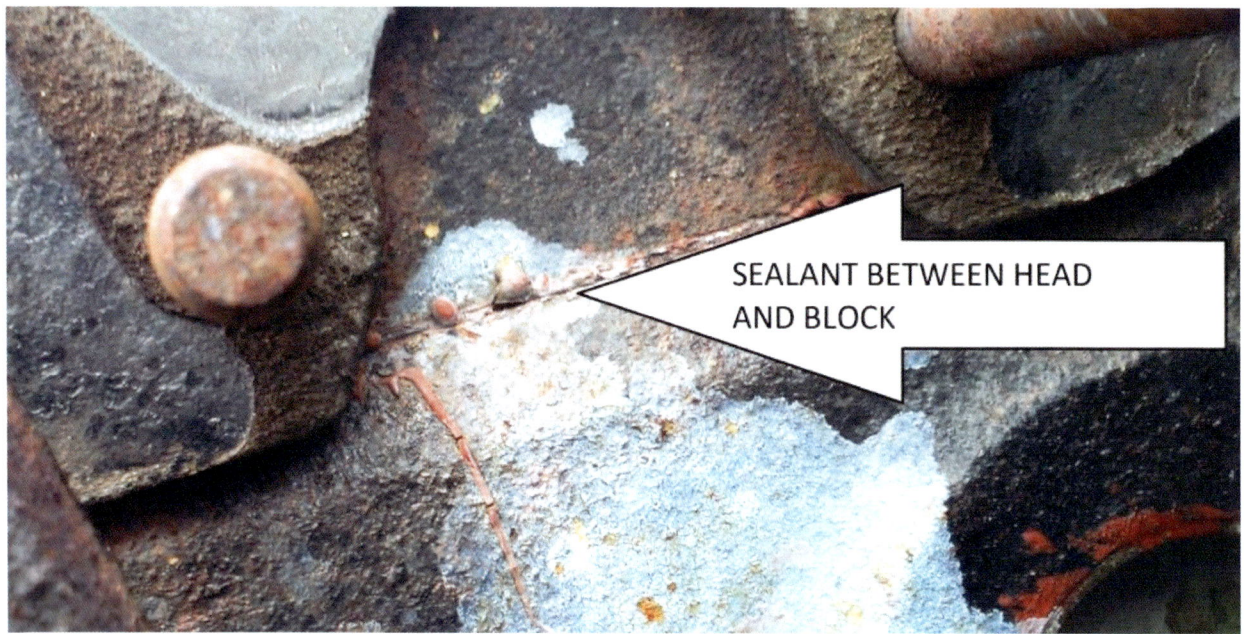

SEALANT BETWEEN HEAD AND BLOCK

unbolted the rocker shaft, then with my torque wrench set at 40 ft lb I checked to see if any of the head bolts would turn, worryingly 4 of the nuts actually undid which meant that they had either never been torqued down to the correct value or hadn't been re torque'd after a running in period, this could have caused the head to warp. I found that only 2 of the remaining 10 nuts were the correct torque, also I could see evidence between the head and block that some type of sealing compound (possibly red Hematite) had been used; this was only visible on the manifold side after the removal of the manifolds.

The push rods were removed and labelled up in the order that they had been taken out.

I tried to lift the head off the block but it was solid and showed no sign that it would come away so using 2 head nuts locked together I removed the 7 studs that had been covered by the rocker cover, the other 7 would not budge so after making some "funnels" out of putty around each stud I filled these funnels with release fluid and gave each stud a tap with a copper mallet in the hope that it would disturb some of the corrosion that I envisaged being present and allow the ingress of the release fluid.

Two days later I once again locked 2 nuts onto the remaining studs and tried to remove them, they wouldn't budge and were stripping the threads, as I wouldn't have wanted to use these studs again I welded nuts onto them and was finally able unscrew the studs, with the studs removed the head came off and revealed a very grotty head gasket with evidence of sealant having been used!

The head was then placed upside down on a bench and with the spark plugs fitted the combustion chambers were filled with a light oil, within half an hour 5 of the inlet valves were leaking oil into the ports, over night one of the exhaust valves had leaked oil into its port.

To check the cylinder bores I used my telescopic gauges and vernier micrometer and measured each bore with each piston at the bottom of its stroke to allow me to measure top and bottom of the bore, I took measurements from front to rear and from side to side with the following results –

	Bottom Front to Rear	Bottom Left to Right	Top Front to Rear	Top Left to Right
Cylinder 1 -	2.9615"	2.9615"	2.9614"	2.962"
Cylinder 2 -	2.961"	2.9625"	2.9615"	2.9615"
Cylinder 3 -	2.961"	2.9615"	2.963"	2.9615"
Cylinder 4 -	2.9615"	2.962"	2.9615"	2.9615"
Cylinder 5 –	2.9615"	2.9615"	2.962"	2.9615"
Cylinder 6 –	2.9615"	2.9625"	2.9615"	2.9615"

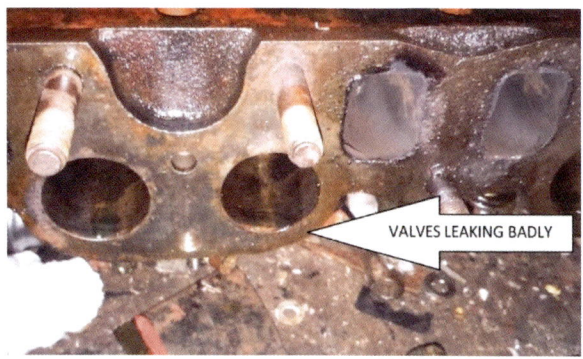

VALVES LEAKING BADLY

The standard bore of a Triumph 2000 is 74.7mm which is 2.9609", therefore the block had been bored out to 0.020" oversize (this was verified when I cleaned up the piston crowns to see + 20"). I measured the stroke of the crankshaft which was the correct 76mm.

I then checked the cylinder head and block face using an engineer's straight edge and feeler gauges to see if they had warped, surprisingly enough, they hadn't!

As a few days had now passed by I found that all the valve seats had leaked apart from the exhaust valve on number 6, so *hopefully* the engine issues were due solely to valve problems and possible cylinder head leakage.

As the bores were showing a maximum of 0.0016" wear and there were no score marks in the bores to denote piston ring damage it was worth the risk of just reconditioning the cylinder head to see if the compressions could be increased, although worn piston rings and or pistons could also be an issue and apart from checking for any movement of them in the bores the only way to check them properly would be to remove them. As it would only cost the price of a head gasket set to fit the cylinder head and test the

engine and the valves were so bad the owner decided that he wanted me to recondition the cylinder head and test the engine.

When I removed the valves I found that the inlet valves on number 4 and number 5 combustion chambers were very tight in their valve guides. When I checked the valve stems they were slightly bent. After cleaning the combustion chambers I found that hardened valve inserts had been fitted to the exhaust valve seats for unleaded fuel, but that all of the valve seats required re-cutting.

Using my valve seat cutting tool I re faced all 12 valve seats (a good job that it has tungsten carbide inserts as otherwise it would not have re cut the hardened valve seats).

Next I attempted to lap in the valves, but the sealing lips on the valves were too badly pitted and needed re facing. If it had just been one or two valves I would have re faced them using my hand grinder with a mounted grinding point to re face the sealing lip while the valve was spun at high speed in my pedestal drill, but as all 12 were in need of attention I called GB Classic Cars and with TSSC discount it was about the same price to buy new valves as it was to have the old ones re faced at the local engine machine shop! Also next day delivery was guaranteed instead of a "we should be able to fit them in at the end of next week" from the machine shop.

Another issue raised its head while I was checking the push rods, one was very slightly bent (I told the owner and he confirmed that this had been the one that had "jumped off" the rocker arm), as the engine was an early Mk II the push rods were unavailable to buy new. It took me quite a few phone calls to my various contacts before I could procure a good second hand one.

As promised by GB Classics the valves arrived the next day along with 7 new cylinder head studs, a new thermostat, 14 new cylinder head nuts and some new valve split collets (some of the old ones were badly scored and had "lips" near the tops). The Payen head gasket set was on back order (other makes available, but I wanted to fit one which I could be confident was of a good quality).

Using coarse, then fine lapping paste all the valves were lapped, I found that the new inlet valves in combustion chambers 4 and 5 were a tight fit in the valve guides (had these caused the old valves to bend?) so I reamed the guides until a nice sliding fit was obtained. The valve springs were all within tolerance so they were all re fitted with new valve collets where needed. The cylinder head was then placed upside down on the bench and the combustion chambers were filled with diesel oil, after 4 hours there was no sign of any leakage from the valve seats.

So with the cylinder head and engine block faces scrupulously cleaned the head was reunited with the block. After all the head components were fitted and torqued down all the ancillaries were also fitted. As there was a danger that coolant had got into the engine oil when removing the head I then drained the engine oil, the filter (which was the spin off canister type) was well and truly stuck to the conversion adapter so it was easier to unbolt the adapter and take the filter off on the bench. It was just as well that I did this as when I removed the adapter I could not believe the amount of emulsified oil that had somehow been trapped in the filter housing and filter.

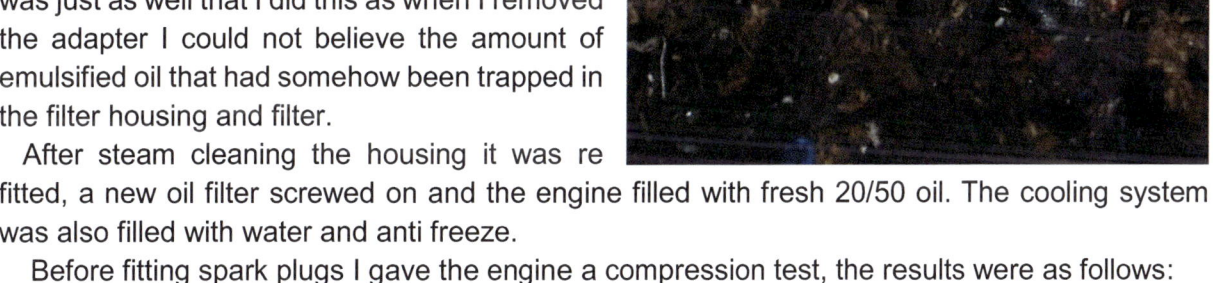

After steam cleaning the housing it was re fitted, a new oil filter screwed on and the engine filled with fresh 20/50 oil. The cooling system was also filled with water and anti freeze.

Before fitting spark plugs I gave the engine a compression test, the results were as follows:

CYL 1 = 130 PSI
CYL 2 = 145 PSI
CYL 3 = 145 PSI
CYL 4 = 145 PSI
CYL 5 = 130 PSI
CYL 6 = 130 PSI

A lot better than before and only just outside the 10% difference that is ideally wanted between values, but these could alter for the better (or worse) after the engine has run for a while as the piston rings may have been sticking slightly.

The engine only turned over slowly, but it started and sounded quite nice, after running it for a few minutes it was allowed to cool down and then another compression test was carried out with the following results –

CYL 1 = 140 PSI
CYL 2 = 148 PSI
CYL 3 = 148 PSI
CYL 4 = 150 PSI
CYL 5 = 142 PSI
CYL 6 = 144 PSI

The car was then taken for a test drive and "went like a rocket" to quote the driver, with no sign of a miss fire.

It might be that the engine would have to come out for new pistons and rings (and very likely a crank regrind), but at least the owner could now plan for this and would have the use of his car until then.

SECTION 3 Gearbox and Clutch

Conversion of Triumph TR4A from Non-Overdrive Gearbox to Overdrive Gearbox

My 4A did not have an overdrive gearbox when I bought it, Overdrive was one of the things that I "sacrificed" from my must have list when I was looking to buy a 4A due to the scarcity of cars within my budget at the time. I knew that once I had a TR4A I could always retro fit an overdrive gearbox and the money that I had acquired partially through selling my totally rebuilt Spitfire (which was the first "it's your Triumph" feature in Triumph World magazine) would be squandered on a new kitchen or bathroom if I took too long to find an acceptable TR4A. I think that most of us have been there once or twice!

At the TR International in Malvern 2010 I bought a reconditioned gear box with a J type overdrive for a bargain price of £750 (you can double that price these days) and below is the description of the installation. From notes (which I have tried to convert into a script that makes sense) that I made at the time I have included the approximate time that each stage took, the work was carried out in my garage using tools that are readily available and that are found in most domestic garages. I will also add the dates on which the work was carried out.

I know that the methods that I used are not always as the workshop manual would endorse, but they worked for me and we all have our own ideas and ways of working which is more often than not dictated by the environment in which we have to carry out the work on our cars.

One of the things that surprised me was the fact that the J type overdrive gearbox was the same overall length as my standard four speed gearbox, which meant that I could use my existing prop shaft.

02/09/2006 8:45 am

13/09/2010

First to be removed were the seats, carpets, radio, H support, gear lever and gear box cover in readiness for the over drive conversion.

I then fitted my original TR4A gearlever to the overdrive gearbox to ensure that it was the correct type as the new gearbox came without a gear lever, it was.

1.75 hours

14/09/2010

I bought a Hamer car lift a few years ago and have found it a great aid when working on my cars, I therefore lifted the TR so that the door bottoms were about waist height.

The speedo cable was removed from the gearbox along with the exhaust centre pipe, starter motor, clutch slave cylinder and clutch inspection cover and the lower bell housing to engine bolts from underneath the car.

A trolley jack was used (placed on a steel bridging piece across the lift's tracks) with wooden blocks to support the rear of the engine and a plank of wood placed across the car lift tracks with blocks to support the gear box.

From inside the car I disconnected the gearbox from the prop shaft and removed the rest of the bell housing to engine bolts/studs.

From under the car I levered the gear box backwards while my friend Veg (not a miss spelling, but when we used to go out pubbing he would usually have to sit in my kitchen for a few hours with various packs of frozen vegetables on the black eyes he had accumulated) pulled the gearbox clear of the engine from inside the car.

Next I lifted the gear box from the car. The new gearbox did not come with the clutch actuating shaft, fork or cover for the input shaft bearing, these had to be taken off the old gear box. On inspection of the old gear box it could be seen that the clutch fork had been welded to the shaft meaning that the assembly could not be removed, this is a known weak point on TR's as the tapered bolt can come loose and cause the hole in the shaft to elongate or even fall out, thus losing clutch action), I checked to see if the parts were available new and as they were I ordered them. An alternative would have been to hacksaw through the shaft to enable removal and then grind through the welds to release the fork, I would have then had to have made a new shaft. The cover from the input shaft bearing was removed and bolted to the new gear box.

As I now had to wait for the parts I was not able to immediately fit the new gear box (a shame as my friend was going back to France, where he is known as Lesgume, the next day) I started to make and fit the over drive electrical circuit using a relay and installing the over drive switch and steering column cowl that I had bought.

5 hours

16/09/2010

The new cross shaft, fork, spring and tapered bolt arrived early afternoon. The hole in the cross shaft had to be taper reamed out to get the correct fit of the tapered bolt, another time when being a former Toolmaker came in handy as I still posses taper reamers among my toolmaking equipment. After that I installed the cross shaft assembly and after bolting a new clutch to the flywheel, using a clutch aligning tool and installing a new thrust bearing, lifted the gearbox into the car. I tried to fit the new rear gearbox mount to the gearbox, but I had to drill out the holes and remove some metal to get it to fit, I then had to cut about 5mm from each side of the car's gear box rear mount locating member to allow the gearbox mounting bracket to fit properly and then I had to open up the holes with a slightly larger drill so that the mounting bolts could be fitted.

The gearbox was then manoeuvred into position with it supported from underneath by the wood across the lift's tracks. I aligned it by eye and slid it into position, with a few light taps on the bell housing with my hide mallet while twisting the output flange with the gears engaged it slipped into place. A number of bell housing to engine nuts and bolts were then installed.

NOTE – the bell housing must have a slightly thicker wall than the original as I could not get a socket on some of the bolt heads, I had to use an open- ended spanner!
4 hours

17/09/2010

I fitted the clutch slave cylinder then found that the rod was too long (probably made that way to compensate for the fork being welded out of position on the clutch cross shaft, I thought – wrong!) so I measured the amount and cut it off. I also fitted a return spring to the cross shaft arm that had not been on the car since I had it. I then installed the flywheel cover and new high torque starter motor. Next I removed the HT lead from the coil, connected the positive to the battery and checked to see it the starter turned the engine over, it did.

After making sure that all nuts and bolts holding the gear box and engine were tight I refitted the front section of the exhaust, I would have to make a new central exhaust bracket as the old one was connected to the old rear gear box mount and will not fit on the new one.

The gear box output shaft was bolted to the prop shaft and the gear box filled with SAE80/90 gear oil, it did not take the full 2 litres so I would check the level after running the car and letting the oil settle.

The car was started and I let it warm up to harden the exhaust sealing paste.

Note : I had bolted the clutch slave cylinder to the wrong side of the mounting plate (as it had been before: my fault for not consulting a workshop manual.) If this is moved to its correct position in the future a longer pushrod will have to be used.
4 hours

20/09/2010

I made an exhaust mounting bracket to attach the exhaust to the gear box rear mount and painted it black.

The two cables that connect the gearbox switch and solenoid were bound together with loom tape and temporary connections were made to the gearbox to check if the new circuit energised the solenoid when in 3rd and 4th gear with the over drive steering column switch made. At first I could select over drive in every gear, I found the cause to be the gear box switch to be permanently made when screwed fully in, I swapped this switch for the other one (one is for the reverse light on a TR6 which I will not be using as I don't have reverse lights) and the circuit worked perfectly. Again showing that just because a part is new, it doesn't necessarily mean that it is any good!

2 hours

21/09/2010

Next I attached the exhaust mounting bracket and fed the cables for the gearbox switch and solenoid through the chassis rails and tie wrapped them to the rear brake line. I cut the cables to length and soldered insulated female spade connectors to them, tested the circuit to see if the solenoid operated when third and fourth gear were selected while the over drive switch was engaged, it did.

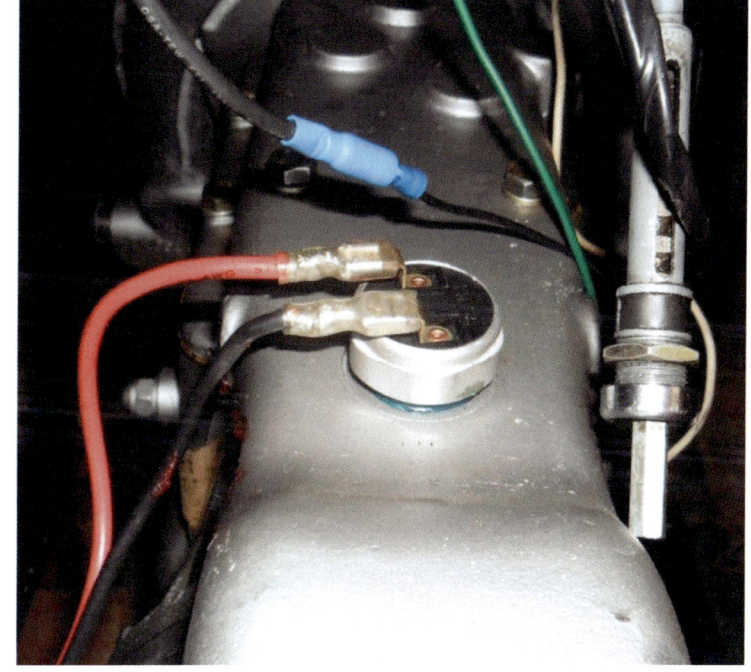

I then made a bracket to thread the two cables through to keep them from fouling the gearbox output flange and painted it black.

After the paint dried I bolted the bracket in position and attached the cables to the solenoid and gearbox switch.

The fibreglass gearbox tunnel that I had bought previously was trial fitted, as it was more rigid than the original cardboard one it was a pain to manoeuvre into position. I marked the position of the holes that I needed to drill in the tunnel as best as I could from under the car, then measured/estimated where the remaining holes should be drilled. The tunnel was removed and I drilled the holes, trial fitted it again and one or two holes had to be opened up/filed slightly to line up with the captive nuts in the car's floor. Trial fitted it again and all was well so I removed the tunnel and used silicone to glue the seal in place on the tunnel.

4 hours

22/09/2010

I glued old carpet underlay to the underneath of the gear box tunnel and fitted the angled speedo drive that I had kept from a scrap Spitfire to the gear box, then found I had to fit a shorter speedo cable which fortunately I had because I had experimented with various length cables on the Herald when fitting an overdrive gearbox to that in the past.

I checked and topped up the gear box oil level then fitted the gear box tunnel. Next to be fitted was the driver's seat and I then lowered the car lift and took the car for a 2 mile run, the over drive was operating as it should on 3rd and 4th gears!

The final job was to fit the "H" section, I had to undo the upper switch console and fitting it all back together took over an hour, what a horrible bloody job! The next time I remove the "H" section I would remove the vinyl covering and file the legs so that it is a looser fit on the gear box cover, it is probably so tight because the new fibreglass tunnel is rigid and probably made over size as most GRP/fibreglass panels are. I then replaced the carpets and seats.

Note: Remove material from 'H' section legs when it is next removed.

3 hours (23.75 hours in total)

I have now been using the car with the overdrive gearbox for over 10 years and touch wood, there have been no problems. Anyone that has driven a car with an over drive knows it makes a tremendous difference on motorways and cruising long distances, I used my TR to travel regularly from my home in Cardiff to our caravan in West Wales and with the price of fuel I rapidly recovered the cost of the over drive gearbox, also as I did not have to part exchange my old gearbox I may one day install it along with a six cylinder Triumph 2000 engine that I have in either my 13/60 or another car that comes my way, maybe even my Vignale!

Whether 6 cylinders or 4 a TR is more ! (especially one with an over drive gear box)

D Type Overdrive Issue

Although the subject car is a Spitfire Mk IV the problem it had was an issue with a reconditioned D type over drive gearbox that had recently been installed and many TRs and other Triumphs have D type over drive units.

The owner had been looking for an over drive gearbox to help keep his Spitfire's engine revs down on motorway journeys and when his standard four speed unit started jumping out of gear he bit the bullet and bought a reconditioned overdrive gearbox from a reputable supplier. As his free time was at a premium he asked if I would start the work on a Friday and he would come and help me to finish it off on the Saturday as he was keen to be involved.

On the Friday after disconnecting the battery and placing the car on 4 axle stands I removed the passenger seat, H section, carpet, gearbox tunnel, gear lever, propshaft (exhaust in the way so that had to come off too), clutch slave cylinder, starter motor and finally the gearbox (basically the same method as a TR). Part of the transmission tunnel was then cut away to accommodate the longer over drive/gearbox unit that was to be fitted. The clutch had only been in the car for a few thousand miles so that was remaining in place, the over drive gearbox being heavier and bigger than the standard one was more difficult to manoeuvre into place but I managed it with a scissor jack supporting the engine and a trolley jack helping me to get the gear box in place. After the gear box was bolted in place I fitted the new shorter propshaft. All electrical connections were then made with the supplied relay secured to the front of the bulkhead. The gearbox had been supplied with all cables, connectors, switch and relay as well as the propshaft and everything looked to be of a very good quality, I was suitably impressed. I filled the gearbox with oil and after checking that the solenoid activated with the gearlever in 3rd and 4th with the ignition on and the gear lever switch in the "in" position I decided to call it a day at that point and to finish it off with the owner as arranged the next day.

Morning came and the owner and I fitted the exhaust, slave cylinder and starter motor and he took the car for a test drive. Fifteen minutes later he returned, "there is something wrong, its very noisy" he said. "That's probably because the tunnel and carpet aren't fitted" I said, "did the overdrive kick in and out?" "Yes" he said, so I placed the tunnel over the gearbox and said "try

that". He did and returned 10 minutes later looking very happy "Fantastic!" he said. So we fixed the gearbox cover in place, then the H section, carpet and passenger seat and he took it for another run and returned looking even happier. I had a drive and was very impressed by the gearbox and overdrive.

Roll forward 6 weeks and he called me to say that the overdrive was "dropping" in and out all the time and would I have a look at it. As most people do, I checked to see if the solenoid was operating every time the switch was operated with the car in both 3rd and 4th gears and it was so I thought it best to remove the H section support and the gearbox tunnel and carpet to check all the electrical connections and switches, they were all good and doing what they should be. Next I checked the oil level and that was still spot on so I removed the cover to expose the "valve actuating arm" to find it adjusted correctly (the hole in the arm lined up with the hole in the casting) but found that when the overdrive was switched off the arm was not always returning to the off position.

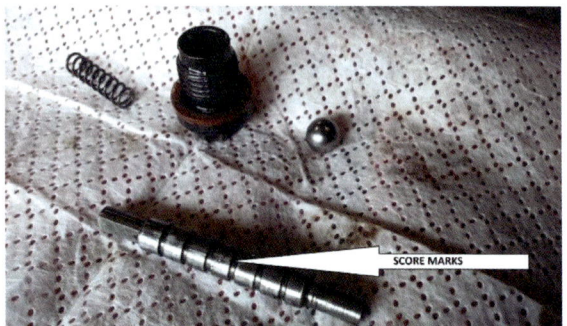

SCORE MARKS

I removed the valve securing nut, spring, top hat plunger and valve to see if any foreign matter (perhaps from when the unit had been reconditioned) was causing the valve to stick and found a few very slight marks on the valve so very carefully using 1200 grade wet or dry sand paper I polished them out.

With the valve re fitted the actuating arm returned to the "out" position every time. Before refitting the gear box tunnel, carpet and H section I took the car for a test drive and the overdrive operated perfectly. The problem that the owner had of the overdrive "dropping" in and out must have been due to the valve sticking as 12 months on it was still working perfectly.

HOLE IN OPERATING ARM MUST LINE UP WITH THE HOLE IN THE CASTING

ADJUSTING NUT

Whether a TR or Spit Mk IV an Overdrive is more!

Triumph TR6 Clutch Bodge

Thursday 7th July, my telephone rings "I've been given your phone number by a friend who says you may be able to help me, my clutch has gone and I'm due to catch the ferry to France for Classic Le Mans later on today!" I took his address which was about 20 miles from my house and went to have a look. On inspection it seemed that play had occurred between the clutch cross shaft and the tapered bolt (probably the hole had elongated over time) which had caused the slave cylinder piston to extend to the very end of the cylinder body (there was no circlip to stop the piston doing this on the type of slave cylinder that was fitted) this had resulted in the seal becoming damaged as it came into contact with the aluminium corrosion and other crud which had built up at the end of cylinder bore and was seeping fluid. There was not enough time to remove the gear box to check so I suggested a "bodge" that would probably last until he returned from Le Mans. I did point out that the tapered bolt *could* fall out at any time *if* it had broken which was possible but in this instance not likely. He was prepared to take the risk because as it was, he wasn't going anywhere and he could always get home on a recovery wagon if he made it to Le Mans. A quick phone call to Lazarus Cars to confirm that they had a new slave cylinder in stock and the TR owner was on his way to Newport to collect it while I put the TR on axle stands and removed the old slave cylinder. To take the extra play out of the clutch action the push rod can be extended, but I did not have my welder with me or any materials that could be used to do this so I bolted the new slave cylinder to the other side of the mounting to where it should be bolted, this was still not enough to give a "good" pedal after bleeding the system although gears could be selected so I placed some thin washers between the slave cylinder and the mounting plate. With the system bled again the clutch action was excellent and a happy chap test drove his TR.

He phoned me the next day to say that he had arrived safely at Le Mans and that the clutch had operated perfectly, he also called me on his return to say that the car was showing no signs of any clutch trouble and asked if he should risk keeping the TR on the road until October when he would be taking the car off the road for the winter (why?) and have the gearbox removed for a permanent repair to be made. I suggested that he booked the car in somewhere and had it sorted out ASAP over a few days during the week when he wouldn't be using the TR which he did, Lazarus Cars of Newport removed the gearbox to find that the tapered bolt had elongated the hole in the cross shaft which they replaced along with the worn clutch.

I don't recommend this bodge unless as in this case it's an emergency, but it worked out well on this occasion.

SECTION 4 Fuel System

TR4A Throttle Pedal Adjustment

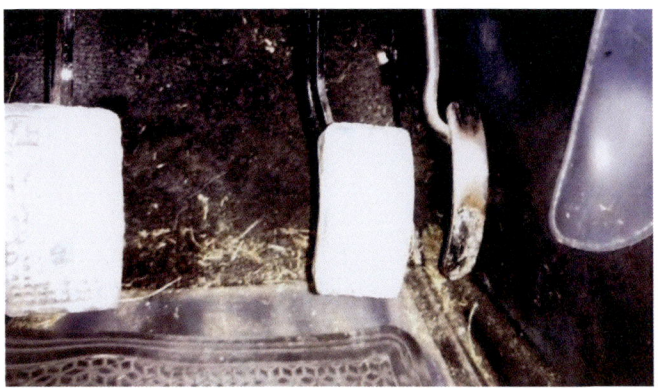

A few years ago I bolstered my TR's driver seat with memory foam to help with the discomfort I had in my right hip on the Classic Le Mans run. The foam made a massive difference, but on longer (than Classic Le Mans runs) I had still been getting a bit of discomfort. Now those who know me and my lack of attention to detail will not be surprised that it has taken me over 15 years to notice that the throttle pedal is lower than the brake and clutch pedals on my TR!

There may be a reason for this and I suppose I could Google it or look on some forums, but some of the "advice" and "facts" that I have seen on the internet are so so so wrong, and I always wonder how many people have incurred serious and sometimes dangerous damage to their cars or to whatever else they are researching. Of course a lot of it is perfectly correct and is a good source of information, but if used , a modicum of experience and common sense should be applied , so another reason for me not to use it, I have no common sense! However, if anyone knows of a reason for a throttle pedal to be lower please let me know, it could be that it has been calculated that a driver is less likely to press on the throttle instead of the brake pedal in an emergency, I just don't know. Anyway, I decided that the fact that I had to push my right leg further to use the throttle pedal may be contributing or even causing the discomfort that I was experiencing so I decided to do something about it. For those who don't know the throttle set up on a 4A it is a series of linkages (as on some other models) and 2 connecting rods, one from the pedal to a cam then a smaller one from the cam to the carburettors link shaft. The connecting rods are threaded at each end and have "ball and sockets", which are adjustable by undoing a locking nut and screwing the ends in the direction which you require.

To bring the throttle pedal up I had to make the longer rod shorter so I undid the locking nuts and screwed the ends in as far as they would go. I then re fitted the rods and found that the pedal had "risen" but not far enough, engaging my engineers brain I calculated that I had to shorten the pedal to cam rod by an inch, so I removed the rod and unscrewed the one end, then I cut an inch off the rod and cut a ¼ UNF thread an inch longer than was left along the rod and screwed the ball and socket fitting back on.

With the linkage rod re installed and re greased the throttle pedal was level with the brake and clutch pedal FANTASTIC!

When I tried the pedal for operation and it felt good, the car revved up as it should and on a road test the car performed as it had previously.

The acid test was a run that I made mid-September 2017 to Bala Lake from Cardiff and back (a 300 mile round trip) taking the A470 up with stops at Rhayader and Dolgellau on the way up, lunch in Bala Town then taking the A494/A458/A49 etc back South with a stop at Ludlow, one of the best drives that takes in both Welsh and English roads. The TR performed faultlessly and was a joy to drive through the beautiful Welsh and English countryside, and my leg, well if I say HIPTASTIC it may give you a clue.

TR4A Carburettor Change

When I bought my TR4A, just as most of the rest of the car, the SU carburettors were very worn. To keep the car running as best as I could until I could afford to replace or recondition them I had packed grease around the spindles to prevent air from being drawn through the spindle bores and altering the state of tune of the carburettors, but I really needed a new or reconditioned pair. While at the TR International in July 2008 I found a carburettor specialist who was willing to sell me a pair of reconditioned carburettors that "were set up for a TR4A and would just bolt on and work" for a knock down show price near the closing time of the event on the Sunday. After ensuring that there was no play in the spindles I duly handed over the cash and looked forward to gaining the benefit of my new purchase. However, when I compared the "reconditioned " carburettors with the ones actually on my 4A I realised that they had "breather" pipes on their bodies, whereas the original ones didn't (my usual no eye for detail flaw), but by then the trader had packed up and gone, I was not too concerned though as they were the right size carburettors.

Below are the notes that I made at the time of fitting and setting up the carburettors along with the dates and the time spent each day just to give you an idea of the timescale this exercise may take you if you are planning a carburettor change.

21/07/2008

I removed old carburettors and installed the reconditioned ones that I bought at the Malvern TR show. I found that the front carburettor float bowl top had the fuel inlet and outlet pipes in different positions and that the choke linkage spindle had a loose spigot and the accelerator linkage spindle was missing the flange that the link arm fits onto. This meant that I would have to fit the old linkage spindles from my original carburettors.

1 ¾ hours

Original carbs in place.

22/07/2008

I set the carburettors with the linkages loose, the car started easily, but then came 3 hours of changing the various rubber fuel pipes, checking the jets were centralised, fitting the old float bowl tops from my original carburettors and cleaning the fuel pump in an attempt to stop fuel from pouring out of the reconditioned carburettors. I wasn't happy and I didn't know if I had completely solved the problem. I needed to buy new fuel pipes. I did drive the car and it seemed to go well.

3 ½ hours

23/07/2008

Today I fitted new fuel pipes, this stopped the leaks. I then tried to tune the carbs, but the engine was still very "lumpy" I was not happy.

2 hours

11/08/2008

I found that one needle was protruding further out of the piston than the other. I filed a radius on the one that was protruding furthest (Piston end) until it sat deeper in the piston and was protruding the same amount as the other one. I then reset the ignition timing, carbs and gave the car a run. It was much better, but not perfect.

I tried using the Spitfire set up of breather pipes from carbs to rocker cover, taking away the need for the ACU valve, but this resulted in the car running roughly, so I reverted to using the standard set up and blocking the new carb breathers.

3 ½ hours

12/08/2008

I fitted new rubber pipes to the carb breather pipes with custom made aluminium plugs in the ends. I then gave the car a run and filled up with petrol, when I got home, the car was running roughly, I found that the rear carb's jet was sticking slightly, so I disconnected the linkage and lubricated it with Vaseline, manually sliding the jet up and down. This seemed to make things better, but then I found that the front carb's jet had stuck.

I was taking the car to west Wales the coming Friday and would see if the carbs bed in a bit (extremely unlikely but time had run out),if not I would have to strip them down and wet or dry any high spots off the jets.

I made a mental note to manually check that the jets were fully home after each cold start.

2 hours

07/09/2008

After driving the TR to West Wales in extremely wet conditions, I found that it returned 24mpg. After checking the spark plug colours I turned the jets up one flat to weaken the mixture.

I took the car on the Pembroke Western Telegraph run on the Sunday, the car returned 26mpg. I covered 318 miles over the weekend and the car performed faultlessly.

After I reconditioned the engine I just could not get the car to run well by altering the mixture and balancing the carburettors, so next is an extract (from my engine rebuild report) from the notes that I made at the time of getting the engine running well after reconditioning it. My apologies if you have already read my engine rebuild report, but it is relevant to my carburettor change/installation and illustrates issues that other non technical people like myself may encounter – you are not alone!

Post Engine Reconditioning

After removing the dashpots I removed the needles and found that they had been fitted so that they were pushed fully home into the bore in the piston (done by myself to get the pre reconditioned engine running properly), as they were the needle type with the shoulder, I re inserted them until the shoulder was flush with the piston face and locked them in position hoping that this would be enough to allow me to lower the jets and still give me a range that would allow me to adjust to the correct mixture. Next I removed the jets and with 1200 wet or dry I "cleaned up" the jets so that they operated smoothly and without sticking when operating the choke. Next I replaced the piston assemblies and dashpots and wound the jets down until they were flush with the bridge and then another 1 ¾ turns. I started the engine and it sounded much smoother so I took it for a 2 mile run then synchronised the carburettors using a carb balancer (I just cannot get it right by using a pipe to my ear, too many years playing drums have taken their toll). I cleaned the spark plugs and then found that I could time the ignition to around 8 degrees BTDC and then just tweak it slightly until the engine tone sounded right (its the only way that I have ever managed to get my engines running well without pinking) I took the car for a 10 mile run, it went beautifully and when I checked the colour of all the spark plugs they were a lovely light brown.

Although I had had issues with the carburettors they had been a bargain buy and the problems that I had setting them up both before and after reconditioning the engine fade into insignificance when I take this into account.

New cbs in place.

72

It's been a few years now since the engine rebuild and I have not had to make any further carburettor adjustments, the car is unbelievably good on fuel and accelerates and drives really smoothly. When I check or change the spark plugs they are always a nice light brown.

Maintaining the "Ball and Socket" Rod End type Carburettor Linkages that connect the accelerator pedal to the carburettors on various Triumph models including TR4 and TR4As

This is a job that I carried out when I replaced the cylinder head on My TR4A in May 2013, but it is the type of job that can be carried out in the depths of winter, at your leisure and after removing the linkages from the car, on your kitchen table.

These linkages can easily be overlooked until one day you remove your foot from the accelerator pedal and the linkages lock or seize, causing your engine to continue to rev and in some cases red line. They are in the vicinity of the exhaust manifold and so are subjected to continuous high temperatures which can dry out any oil or grease that may have been previously applied.

To remove the assembly from the car first of all remove the throttle return springs then undo the ball joint on the rod end that screws in to the accelerator pedal and then the one that bolts onto the shaft that connects two carburettors' butterfly shafts. After that undo the two nuts that fix the assembly to the carburettor mounting flange.

With the assembly removed from the car you can then work on it either on your work bench or kitchen table etc.

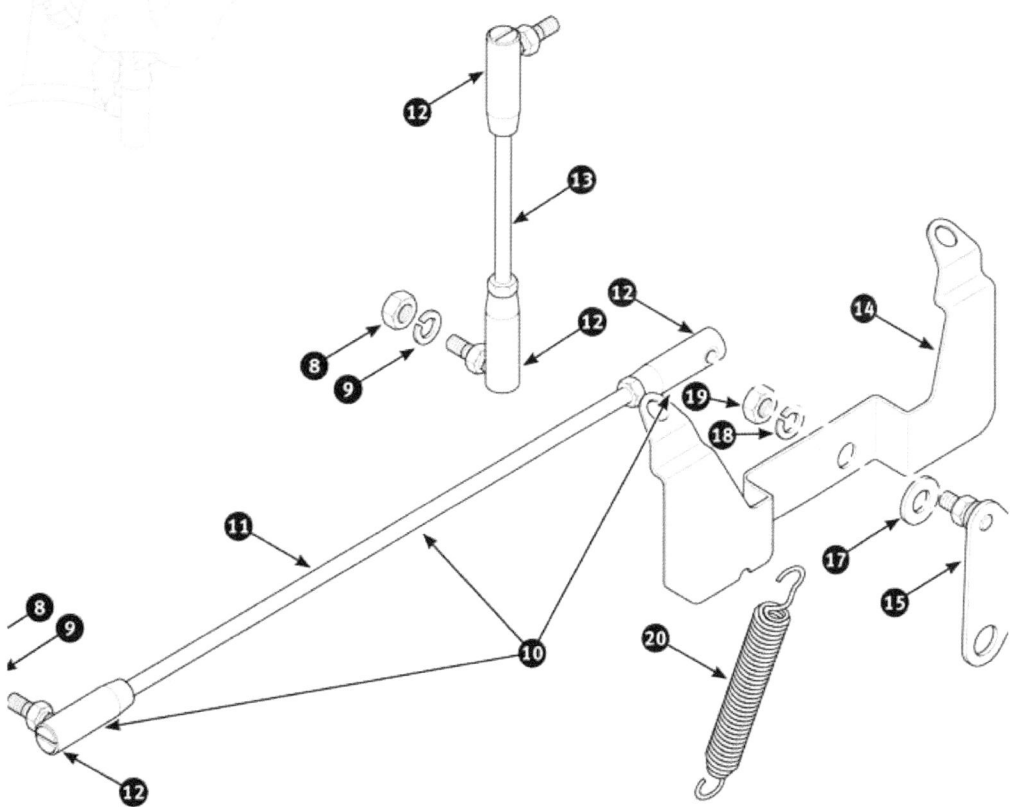

TR4A throttle linkage, rod ends or ball and socket joints are number 12

Working on one ball joint at the time, remove the split pin which will then allow you to unscrew the end cap and withdraw the "ball", you will see that the end cap is shaped to accommodate the ball part of the joint. After thoroughly cleaning the parts, carefully inspect the ball part for wear and roughness, if it is too worn buy replacements, if it is only showing slight signs of wear or slightly rough use a fine grinding stone in a hand held grinder or a very good quality fine file or a diamond file to smooth it down. When this is done re assemble the joint and screw the end cap in until it locks the joint, then back it off gradually until the ball turns freely, if you detect the ball sticking at all, dismantle it and check again for any roughness on the ball. Repeat this until you are satisfied that the ball is sitting nicely in the socket with the end cap slightly backed off, but without too much slack.

Remove the end cap again and lubricate the ball and socket with a copper based grease so that the heat from the exhaust does not dry it out and re assemble. When you are happy that the joint moves freely and is not too slack insert a new split pin to lock the end cap in position.

Repeat this with the other three ball and socket joints and then replace the assembly in the car.

If any of your joints had previously been stiff, dry or slack you should notice a better "feel" to your accelerator pedal.

SECTION 5 Brakes

Brake Calliper Rebuild

Although the callipers used for this article were off a Triumph Stag I was re commissioning for someone, the process is the same for most brake callipers and especially those commonly used on Triumphs, I have reconditioned many Type, 12, Type 14 and Type 16 callipers over the years using this method **when the pistons have been seized solid in the callipers**, once I had to carefully drill and tap holes in the bottom of the pistons after separating the calliper halves, a bolt was then screwed in to "jack" the pistons out, fortunately on this Stag I was able to remove the pistons using a vice after getting the pistons to move out enough for me to be able to grip them .

Method – after applying brake cleaner around the pistons and leaving a few hours for it to soak in I attached my home made brake line/ air compressor hose attachment to the calliper then used a G clamp to prevent the both pistons from being blown completely out, the clamp was adjusted so that the one piston would come against the anvil of the clamp and the other would be prevented from being blown out by the outside curvature of the clamp.

With my brake line/air compressor hose connected to the airline the compressor "tap" was slowly opened and the one piston moved, the other was still solid, so I tapped the calliper body with a brass dolly and the still seized piston moved about 1mm. I kept the calliper under pressure for a few minutes, but even with a few more taps with the dolly there was no further movement so I disconnected the air line then using the clamp I pressed the seized piston fully back after giving it a good dose of release oil .The G clamp was then put back in place and I applied air pressure again, with a few more taps with my dolly the piston moved out about 2mm.

I continued releasing the air pressure, pressing the piston back home then applying air pressure until there was about 12mm of the piston protruding from the calliper (about the same as the opposing piston), then unscrewed my brake line/air compressor hose. Next I undid the bolts holding the calliper halves together (using a torque wrench and noting the amount or torque required to move the bolts) and taking each half in turn, gripped the piston in the vice then using

2 pry bars I eased the calliper half off the piston (being very careful not to lever on the face that mates to the other half of the calliper). This was repeated until all 4 pistons were removed.

The callipers were then cleaned and re assembled using new pistons, seals and O rings that seal the two calliper halves making sure that the mating faces of the callipers were scrupulously clean after using an oil stone to give them an even better mating surface. I tightened the bolts to the same torque that was required to loosen the bolts plus 5 ft/lb to allow for the thread lock that had been on the bolts and used new spring washers and thread lock. I must say that the Stag calliper dust seals were far less fiddly to fit than the type that are held onto the calliper with a spring type clip. The callipers were then checked for leakage by re attaching my brake line/air compressor hose, placing new brake pads in the callipers with a piece of packing between them, turning on the air and placing the calliper in a water bath, any leakage would have produced air bubbles.

You always have to be careful when using compressed air, so if you don't have the proper facilities and equipment it is far safer and more controllable to use a hydraulic pump to remove seized pistons. You will also sometimes be advised that splitting brake callipers is a specialist job, but it is well within the capabilities of anyone with the slightest modicum of engineering sense.

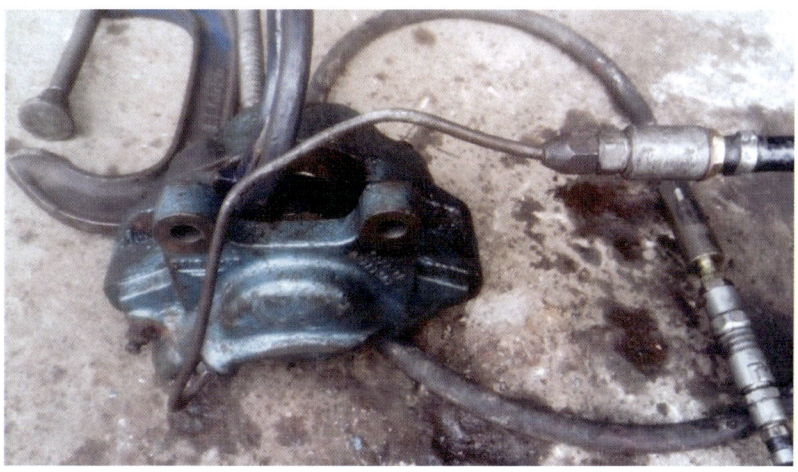

OLD SEAL HAD BEEN DAMAGED WHEN FITTED

THIS O RING SEALS THE 2 HALVES OF THE CALLIPER AND WAS RENEWED

Converting from TR4A fly-off handbrake to conventional set up.

Is it just my Triumphs or does anybody else get the "your handbrake is on the limit" speech at MOT time? My Herald is usually just inside the limit, my Stag Saloon is fine, but my TR4A is usually "on the limit and could do with adjusting" even though it is correctly adjusted. With the TR4A you have the added complication of the system being a "fly off one" (for those who have never used one the method of use is – pull the lever up while holding in the button, relieve the pressure on the handbrake lever while still pressing the button, then take your thumb off the button, to release the handbrake you just pull the lever up slightly without touching the button and let go, the handbrake then disengages for faster standing starts I believe). This makes it awkward to pull the lever to its highest position (for me anyway) and the MOT tester usually has to hold the handbrake lever up to get the required readings. It is also easy to forget the technique when you are constantly using different cars and there have been a few times when I have been stopped at a junction on a hill and I have messed up the handbrake application!

Over the years I have renewed the rear brake wheel cylinders, brake adjusters and brake shoes on both wheels and handbrake cables, but still at MOT time the car only just passes. The actual drums look to be in excellent condition with no wear, but I am conscious that steel surfaces can "work harden" or become "glazed" with use and sometimes with brake drums this can be the cause of poor performance, however, the rear brakes work perfectly and are always at the high end of performance when tested on the MOT rollers. Add to this the issue of forgetting which car I'm in when starting off on a hill and I thought that I would try to convert my TR4A to a conventional set up as on the TR6.

I checked out the part numbers for the TR4A handbrake set up against the TR6. There were only two differences – The TR4A handbrake lever is part # 141688, the TR6 is 148080, The TR4A rod that connects to the button is part # 141688 and the TR6 one is 132588.

I could not find anyone selling these parts new, but I was eventually able to buy the two parts for £30 through a well known internet auction site.

I jacked the rear of the car up, placed axle stands under the chassis, removed the road wheels and with the handbrake applied I used my large torque wrench to see how much torque was needed to turn the hubs and found it to be 68ft lb. I removed the seats and pulled back the carpet to get comfortable access to the handbrake lever and with the hand brake cable disconnected at both wheels I managed to disconnect the cables from the handbrake lever assembly and remove it. I had previously cleaned up the TR6 handbrake lever assembly and given it a coat of black enamel paint. With the ratchet assembly and pivot pin coated in copper grease I connected the handbrake cables and bolted the lever in position. With the cables reattached to the handbrake operating levers at the wheels and adjusted I applied the handbrake. Using my torque wrench again to turn the hubs I noted that the torque needed was about 15% greater at around 82 ft lb!

So now I had a more efficient handbrake and I don't have to worry about messing up a hill start or even rolling back into the car behind as had nearly happened a few times with the fly off system.

When I took the car for its next MOT it passed without any comment from the tester, I asked him how the handbrake was and he replied that it was just over the pass limit, so all in all I am very satisfied with this conversion.

No visible difference from 'fly off' handbrake.

TR Handbrake Lever Extensions

The handbrake on my TR4A had always been a "just passed" whenever I mot'd the car, mostly it was borderline and needed a few "tweaks" to get it through even with new shoes, drums and cables. A few years ago I converted it from the standard "fly off" set up to the more common and more user friendly (for me) standard set up by using TR6 parts, however, although my TR was now passing it's mot's without any handbrake issues, I still had to give it a hefty pull when stopping on steep hills to stand any chance of it holding. I was therefore very interested when I came across Handbrake Lever Extensions advertised on a well known auction site and even though I could have made up a set at my friend's local small engineering company I felt that as it was brake parts I would be better off buying them from a bona fide company who would have carried out the research to ensure that the correct materials for the application would have been used.

And so I purchased a pair and after less than an hour after they arrived they were installed on my TR4A, even after having to adjust the handbrake cables. Before I fitted them I used my torque wrench to turn the rear hubs (raised off

EXTENSIONS IN PLACE

the ground and out of gear) with the handbrake on, the handbrake started to slip at 82ftlb. After I installed the lever extensions I repeated this process and the handbrake showed no signs of slipping when I came to the end of my torque wrench's range which is 100ftlb, so this shows an efficiency increase of over 20%, very handy (pardon the pun).

At the next mot my TR sailed through the mot with the handbrake registering a very healthy reading on the brake rollers.

Whether six cylinders or four a TR is more (especially when its handbrake works)!

TR4A Sticking Rear Brake

My TR4A had on occasions "suffered" from a "sticking" rear N/S brake. I first noticed it after the car had sat with the handbrake on for a few days leading me to think that it was due to the shoes sticking to the drums so when the car was going to be left idle for a while I did not pull up the handbrake (always a good idea anyway), but then he issue occurred sometimes even when I had braked and not even pulled up the handbrake! Time to investigate. With the car jacked up and on axle stands I removed the rear N/S wheel and brake drum, everything looked okay except for the clevis pin that connects the handbrake cable to the aluminium handbrake lever extension, it was seized in both the extension and the handbrake cable bracket.

Clevis pin seized.

I didn't think that this would have caused the problem because there was enough flex in the handbrake cable to allow the shoes to move, but I couldn't find anything else wrong (except for finding heavy corrosion in the bottom of the rear wing/wheel arch, too many days driving it on salted roads in the winter) so I eased out the clevis pin and fitted a new one with plenty of copper slip. After a few run outs in the car the brake hasn't stuck on again so this simple fix seems to have done the trick (we'll see!)

Foot note – since carrying this out I have covered many miles over many runs and the brake hasn't stuck on once, Braketastic!

New clevis pin fitted and lubricated with copper grease.

SECTION 6 Suspension

TR4A Front Suspension Rebuild

When I first bought my TR4A the negotiated price included an agreement for the previous owner to have it mot'd as the car had been off the road for a few years, so I was very surprised when I picked the car up to find that at speeds of over 40mph I couldn't so much as steer the car, but point it in the general direction which I wanted to go. I had driven a few TR4As when I had been searching for one within my limited price range (for a TR that is) so I knew that my car was at fault and that it wasn't a general TR4A quirk! The first thing that I checked was the tension of the wheel spokes (TR4As had wire wheels fitted as standard) which were fine.

As the tyres were quite old and the car had been sat unused in a garage for a year or two these were the first things to be changed, five new tyres and inner tubes later and the car was, still the same!

I checked the steering column for any play and the bushes seemed fine, but with my son Jack turning the steering wheel with the car firmly on the ground I noticed what I would describe as " excessive flexing" of the rubber lower steering column joint. Although these joints were available I thought that a more rigid item would give me a better feel through the steering wheel and would also "tighten up" the car's steering. I did a bit of research and found that a TR6 universal joint type steering column joint would fit and after purchasing one and fitting it I tried out the car. This made a massive difference and I could now steer the car and drive it as a TR should be driven, but as I had made such a big improvement for so little money I decided to continue to try to improve the car's performance by checking out and reconditioning the front suspension. I also carried out a few more jobs like having the bumpers re chromed while the car was off the road. Although the jobs took a few months I was working at the time and only had an hour or so each evening, also there was no point in rushing the job as I had to wait for the bumpers to come back from the chrome platers.

Below is an account in "diary" style to give you an idea of how long the various jobs that made up the rebuild took. I also decided to clean up the brake and clutch master cylinder brackets and the area on the bulkhead where they are situated as there was a lot of damaged paint work from previous fluid leaks or spillage.

14/09/2008

I drove the TR onto my Hamer car lift then jacked the front of the car so that the wheels were off the lift tracks, placed wooden blocks under the chassis and removed the road wheels. I then removed **all** front O/S suspension components.

4 hours

16/09/2008

The suspension components were cleaned up in a parts washer in my then place of employment.

I scraped and wire brushed the front O/S chassis leg and shock absorber/road spring turret back to bare metal and painted them with rust converting paint.

The brake calliper was then cleaned and I gave the one side a coat of blue calliper paint.

2 hours

17/09/2008

Today I installed the new wheel bearings in the front O/S hub then painted the front O/S chassis leg and suspension turret with chassis black paint, the one side of the brake calliper

was given another coat of paint. After that I removed the front and rear bumpers for re chroming.

2 hours

18/09/2008

I wire brushed then painted the bottom front O/S wishbones, mounting brackets, shock absorber bracket and road spring bottom plate then painted all around the front O/S wing to body tub join with black Waxoil.

1 ½ hours

22/09/2008

The bottom front O/S wishbones, mounting brackets, shock absorber bracket and road spring bottom plate were given another coat of paint. The other side of the brake calliper was painted then Waxoil was applied to the inside of the front O/S wing and body tub.

Next I removed the front O/S track rod end and steering rack gaiter.

1 ½ hours

23/09/2008

Today I fitted new bushes to the bottom front O/S wishbones, cleaned and greased the two sets of shims then installed the new "standard TR4A" front O/S road spring complete with bottom bracket and lower wishbones.

The O/S steering rack arm was greased and I fitted a new gaiter.

2 ½ hours

24/09/2008

The brake and clutch pedal assembly along with the clutch and brake master cylinders and brackets were removed. The top O/S wishbones, master cylinder bracket, clutch and brake pedals, disc brake dust cover, wheel hub and vertical link were given a coat of paint.

1 ¼ hours

25/09/2008

The top O/S wishbones, master cylinder bracket, clutch and brake pedals, disc brake dust cover, wheel hub and vertical link were given another coat of paint. The lower wishbone nylon bushes were then installed.

1 ¼ hours

26/09/2008

The next to be assembled were the top wishbones (with new poly bushes) and vertical link. A jack was placed under the bottom wishbones and I removed the road spring compressor.

Next the new shock absorber was installed (after first having to drill out the bottom eye to 7/16" from 3/8" !).

1 ½ hours

03/10/2008

To the front O/S suspension I fitted a new track rod end, tightened all suspension nuts and installed new split pins. The brake disc back plate was then fitted.

1 hour

04/10/2008

I removed the pistons from the O/S brake calliper; although they were in good condition new ones were fitted. I found that the wrong type of dust seal had been supplied with the seal kit that I bought. I had to buy new kits as the old ones were damaged while disassembling.

1 hour

05/10/2008

Today I removed the N/S brake calliper, removed the pistons and sprayed it with degreaser. The front N/S hub and disc brake were then removed.

I then undid the N/S shock absorber top nuts and the four nuts that hold the bottom brackets onto the lower wishbone. The brackets were rusted solid onto the wishbone so I sprayed them with Plus Gas. Plus Gas was also sprayed on all N/S suspension bolts and nuts.

1 hour

10/10/2008

I removed the front N/S shock absorber, top and bottom wishbones, road spring, vertical link and track rod end.

1.25 hours

13/10/2008

I drilled and chiselled out a patch that was welded on the front N/S chassis near the lower rear wishbone mount (vertically) and found a lot of dry corroded filings from the original chassis inside the chassis leg. I removed the filings using a telescopic magnet. I then dressed the edges of the hole and made a template of the shape. There was also a hole in through the back plane of the chassis which I would fill with weld. I didn't paint the patch with weld through primer as I would ensure that the entire inner chassis leg gets an extremely generous coating of wax oil.

1 ¾ hours

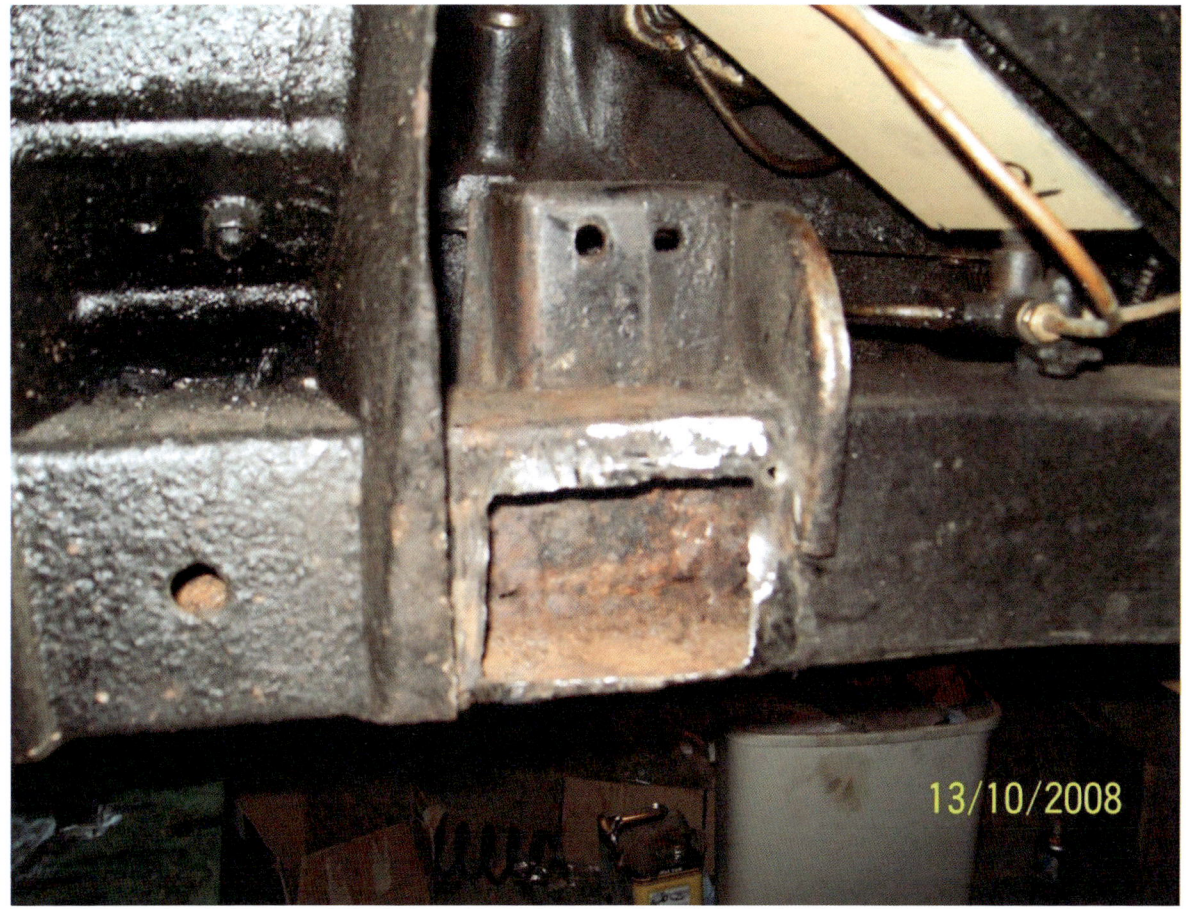

13/10/2008

14/10/2008

I welded in a patch flush to the N/S front chassis. I also welded a patch on the inner vertical face butting against the lower wishbone mount.

1 ½ hours

15/10/2008

I ground down the welds and applied more welds to strengthen the repair. I found that there was a hole (caused by corrosion) on the top of the chassis leg to the left of the lower wishbone mount so I made a patch and welded over the hole and to the wishbone mount (after spraying on weld through primer). As I had found so much corrosion I thought that I would now make a larger strengthening patch to cover the original repair on the front vertical chassis leg, just for peace of mind. The repair was sprayed with weld through primer ready for when I would weld on the over patch.

1 ½ hours

16/10/2008

I made a strengthening patch in work, sprayed it with weld through primer and seam welded it in position. The area was sprayed with stone guard, then I started scrapping the old paint and under seal from the rest of the chassis leg and suspension turret.

1 ½ hours

17/10/2008

Today I cleaned inside the front N/S wing and then painted it with black Waxoil. The front N/S chassis leg and suspension turret were painted with rust killing black paint.

Next I injected the two front chassis legs and suspension turrets with Waxoil.

2 ¼ hours

18/10/2008

Today I painted all the front N/S suspension components including the brake calliper.

1 ¼ hours

19/10/2008

I removed the front N/S steering rack gaiter then gave all the suspension components another coat of paint.

1 ½ hours

20/10/2008

I installed the new "standard TR4A" front N/S road spring and bottom wishbone using new poly bushes.

1 ½ hours

21/10/2008

The front N/S top wishbone with new poly bushes was installed today, The lower trunnion was filled with semi fluid grease and installed on to the vertical link.

1 ¾ hours

22/10/2008

When checking that the brackets for the front N/S lower wishbones were pulled tight against their mountings I found that the rear one had a slight gap near the bottom. It was likely that the bracket was holding off because of the weld on the plate that I had put on the chassis had butted against the mounting.

1 hour

22/10/2008

I removed the front N/S wishbone assembly and relieved the bracket that was holding it off, the wishbone was refitted and I reconnected the vertical link. After this I fitted a new steering rack gaiter to the N/S.

The front O/S shock absorber, lower wishbones, wheel hub and vertical link were removed and poly bushes pressed into the lower wishbones (I had used the nylon type previously by mistake!) and I reassembled the lower wishbones, shock absorber and vertical link.

3 ¾ hours

23/10/2008

It was now time to replace the front O/S wheel hub complete with the new wheel bearings and D washer. The front N/S shock absorber was fitted and while doing so I noticed that there was a gap between the bottom eye and the mounting brackets so I removed the assembly and placed washers between the eye and the mounts then re assembled it all. I checked the O/S and found that there was a gap the one side, so I removed the assembly, placed a washer in the one side then I reassembled it all.

1 ¼ hours

07/11/2008

I installed a new piston, seals and dustcovers in the front O/S brake calliper and installed the assembly complete with the brake pads. The old steel brake pipe that connected the front O/S flexi pipe to the four-way junction on the front N/S chassis leg was removed, I made a new one from copper pipe and installed it.

The front N/S wheel hub complete with new wheel bearings was installed and any excess grease cleaned from the front O/S and N/S suspension.

3.5 hours

08/11/2008

I touched up any scratches that I could see on the front suspension components then masked up the area around the front bulkhead which had previously been painted with a rust treatment and gave it two coats of primer. I then removed the front N/S bumper bracket and the two rear O/S brackets to be shot blasted and repainted

1 hour

09/11/2008

Today the front bulkhead area where the master cylinders are located were given two coats of paint.

½ hour

10/11/2008

I installed one piston in the front N/S brake calliper then gave the bulkhead area another coat of paint. The clutch and brake pedal components were assembled using a new shaft and bushes.

1 ¾ hour

11/11/2008

I replaced the front N/S and rear O/S bumper irons and removed the front O/S and rear N/S ones for de rusting and painting. The second piston was installed in the N/S brake calliper with new seals and dust cover then the calliper was installed.

1 ½ hours

12/11/2008

I made and fitted a copper brake pipe to connect the front N/S calliper to the flexi pipe, cleaned the underneath (drivers footwell) of the bulkhead where the brake and clutch master cylinders locate and painted it with anti corrosion/rust killer paint.

13/11/2008

I installed the clutch and brake pedal assembly complete with master cylinder bracket, clutch master cylinder and new brake master cylinder. I removed the old brake line that linked the master cylinder to four way junction on the front N/S chassis leg and made a new one out of copper pipe and installed it.

2 ¼ hours

14/11/2008

I bled the brake system and made a mental note to check to see if it was OK in a few days time. The steering column was then removed, stripped down, the bushes replaced (even though they felt fine, they fell apart on removal), re assembled and re installed it.

4 hours

15/11/2008

I gave the front O/S and rear N/S bumper irons a coat of black enamel paint. Checked the underneath of the car and touched up any scrapes with Waxoil based under seal. I measured the bottom of the outer steering column so that I could have a custom made collar manufactured, as the original one was missing (if there ever was one).

½ hour

21/11/2008

Today I installed the collar that I had made on the outer steering column then tightened all clamps. The front O/S and rear N/S bumper irons were fitted. Next to be fitted was the front splined wheel hubs and road wheels. The car was lowered back onto its wheels, the front end was looking a bit too high for my liking, but in the very unlikely event that the suspension would "settle" I left it as it was.

1 ½ hours

12/12/2008

The bumpers finally came back from plater's so I painted the inner surfaces of the two bumpers and front over riders with black enamel paint.

¾ hour

18/12/2008

Before I could fit the bumpers I found that I had to open up most of the bolt holes as they had "closed up" with layers of chrome plate.

¼ hour

20/12/2008

I fitted the front bumper, over riders and badge bar then loosely bolted the rear bumper and over riders in place.

½ hour

22/12/2008

Today I completed the fitting of the rear bumper and then fitted the front number plate. I tried to start the car, but found that I had to work out where the electronic ignition feed had been before I had disconnected it. I also found that I had not refitted the alternator plug. When I had sorted this out the car started.

2¼ hour

23/12/2008

I took the car for a drive through about 7 miles of lanes to see if the front suspension settled to a lower level. It didn't, I decided to use the car as it is for a while then look at finding lower front springs or putting the old ones back in.

The front suspension never did settle to an acceptable height so after a few weeks of driving the car, I removed the new "standard TR4A front springs" and replaced them with the original re painted ones. The car now looks "right" and now actually handles and steers as a well set up TR4A should.

After many years the chassis is still solid.

Author's son Jack with the TR, reunited with its original springs.

New Trunnion for TR6

My friend Chipmunk's TR6 had an advisory concerning slight play in one of the lower Trunnions (there was a spate of these in S. Wales, probably due to the state of the roads), he removed the Trunnion and found that the Vertical link was excellent, but there was slight play in the lower brass Trunnion (he will have to use semi fluid grease from now on, in fact grease might have taken up the play). Chipmunk bought a Trunnion for a very reasonable £32, but as he was working away from home and he wanted the car for the weekend he asked me to fit it for him.

I have always checked the ability of Trunnions to hold oil before I fit them as many years ago I installed one on my Spitfire and the next day I found a small pool of SAE90 under the road wheel (it wouldn't have been a problem if I had been using semi fluid grease at that time). The best way to do this is to fill them up with water and leave overnight to see if any leaks out through the blanking disc that is inserted after the internal "thread" has been machined. If it holds water it will hold oil, it may even hold oil if it allows water to escape due to the oil's viscosity, but leaks only ever get worse so it is best to resolve the issue properly. Anyway, Chipmunk's Trunnion was half empty when I inspected it after a few hours so out came my blow lamp and after coating the join between the Trunnion body and the disc with flux I warmed the Trunnion up until the solder flowed freely around the join making a nice seal. Another way of doing this is to add some sealant like Wellseal into the bottom of the Trunnion and allow it a few hours to find any leaks before you fit

the Trunnion, you can also use the two methods if you are unsure of your soldering capabilities. After leaving the Trunnion full of water overnight I checked t see if any had leaked out, none had.

With this done I ¾ filled the Trunnion with SAE90 (Chipmunk's preferred lubricant) and reassembled the Trunnion. I would urge anyone who is replacing a Trunnion on any model of car to test its ability to hold oil as even the slightest seep will soon empty your Trunnion (if you are using oil), leaving you in danger of suffering a broken joint with the potential of a bad accident.

I contacted the supplier of the Trunnion; to let them know and they had been unaware of any issues and had sold many in the past, but the chap I spoke to was extremely knowledgeable and friendly and he assured me that there had not been any other instances so Chipmunk might have just been unlucky, or the previous buyers had not checked. The one that had leaked on my Spitfire all those years ago had been a genuine Stanpart item so this article is in no way intended to infer that the supplier of Chipmunk's Trunnion is in any way inferior and I am extremely glad that we can rely on them to continue sourcing and supplying parts to keep our cars on the road.

Conversion of TR4A from Lever Arm Rear Suspension to Telescopic Damper.

Here is an account (as accurate as I can recall using notes made at the time) of the conversion to a rear shock absorber set up from the original lever arm arrangement that I carried out on my TR4A in late 2006/early 2007. I used adjustable shock absorbers to enable me to alter the "ride" of the car should I need to do so. So far the conversion has proved to be excellent and I have never regretted carrying it out even though it gave me problems at the time. I bought the conversion kit from a well-known TR specialist and when I did incur the problem that I did, I contacted them and they said that they had not had any other reports of problems with the conversion kit, they were even generous enough to offer to carry out the conversion for me on a labour free basis if I took the car to them. It would have been easy enough to re fit the lever arms and drive the car to them, but I wanted to sort it out myself. I thought at the time that it may have been just a couple of rogue brackets that I had bought, or it may have been an issue specific to my car, although the latter was not likely, it may even be that there are TR4As – TR6s out there that have had this conversion and the issue hasn't raised its head as the rear suspension will probably never travel enough for the damper/shock absorber to foul the trailing arm under any driving condition (I have since worked on 2 TR6s that have had this conversion and the dampers foul the trailing arms well before full suspension travel is achieved!), so if anyone who has carried out this conversion on their car has ever heard a "clunk" that they haven't found the cause of , it may be worth just checking it out by raising your road wheels off the ground and checking out the full travel of your trailing arms.

14/12/2006
I drove the TR onto my Hamer lift and raised the lift to its full height and after jacking the rear of the car up from the lift tracks I placed blocks under the chassis and lowered the car onto the blocks so that the rear wheels were clear of the lift tracks.
1/2 hour
15/12/2006
I removed the rear damper units and both the rubber bump stops, to do this I had to drill out the stud on the O/S before the rubber cone mounting would come undone and I had to drill and re tap the N/S rubber cone mounting holes.
1 hour
19/12/2006
I cleaned and scraped all loose under seal from the areas underneath the rear of the car and I painted rust converter on any area that had surface rust.
1 hour
21/12/2006
Today I applied another coat of rust converter and then gave the differential a good brushing with degreaser and drained the oil. Then I gave both trailing arms a good brushing with degreaser. After I had cleaned the differential and trailing arms I repeated the process as there was 40 years of road grime to get rid of.
1 hour
27/12/2006
All areas that had been treated with rust converter were painted and when dry were given a good coat of Waxoil enriched under seal.
1 hour

28/12/2006

Today I installed the two brackets that are used to convert the car to telescopic damper suspension from the original lever arm set up. There was no drilling involved as they locate on the mounting holes that the lever arm dampers had used, so the car can always be converted back to original specification. When they were fitted along with the shock absorbers I found not only that the shock absorbers fouled on the trailing arms thus impeding the travel of the suspension, but they were also rubbing the sides of the mounting brackets near the top and this was without the weight of the car on them. This was very annoying as I had had the brackets zinc plated for corrosion protection and now I had to cut and weld the brackets in order to get them to allow the suspension to function correctly and to reduce their thickness at the top to prevent the shock absorbers from rubbing on them(I know, my fault for not checking them out before, a mistake I have learnt from, but in my defence I had the brackets zinc plated as a favour which could only be offered within a short space of time and not extended to when I would be carrying out the conversion).

1 hour

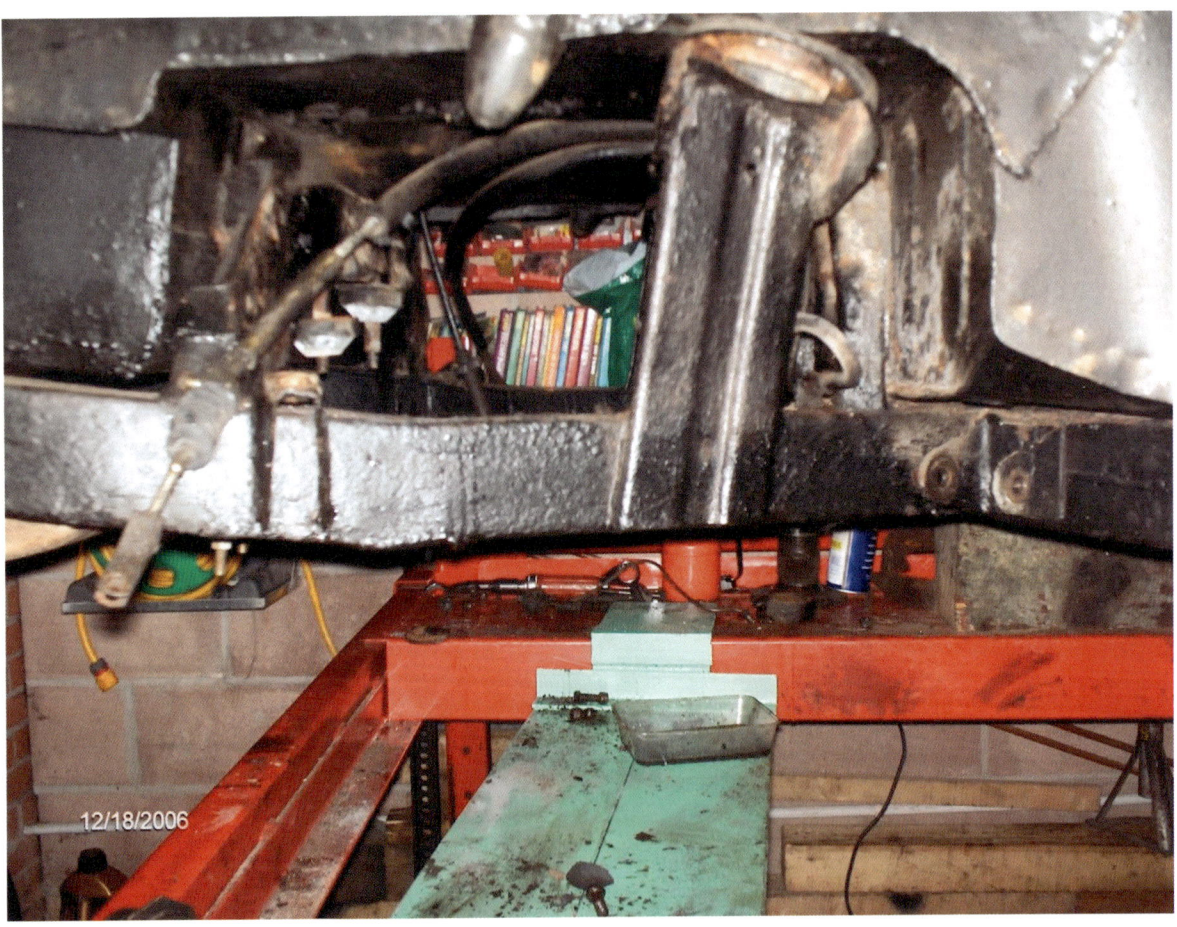

BRACKETMADE NARROWER FOR DAMPER CLEARANCE

01/20/2007

02/01/2007

By repeatedly fitting and removing the telescopic damper conversion brackets, cutting off the top mount and removing metal where the brackets fouled the dampers I was able to mark out the position where the top mountings would need to be welded to allow the full travel of the suspension without the trailing arms fouling against the dampers. I then tack welded them in place and trial fitted them and this time the dampers did not foul the trailing arms. I then removed the brackets and using an arc welder I finish welded the brackets and added strengthening fillets for good measure. The brackets were then given a few coats of enamel paint and after drying they were bolted into position. I cannot emphasise enough that you should only carry out welding work on components that bear weight or have anything to do with safety on your car if you are a fully competent welder, I was trained in all aspects of welding as an apprentice even to the level of being a coded welder so I know how to ensure maximum weld strength and penetration, I mention this because in my years of working on cars I have come across many "welds" which have looked good, but which have come apart with little pressure applied to them, if in doubt tack weld your components together and then take them to an engineering works or competent garage for professional welding.

3 ½ hours

03/01/2007

After fitting the N/S bump stop and shock absorber I found that the shock absorber "bottomed out" before the radius arm hit the bump stop! To get over this problem I made an extension for

99

the bump stop which I replicated for the O/S. The differential was then filled to it's correct level with oil.

1 ½ hours

It was now time to test the car to see how the rear suspension had been affected. After a few miles taking bends steadily my confidence grew and I started to drive a bit quicker into the bends, I found that the car hugged the road better than the old lever arm set up and vastly improved the car's handling even though the lever arm dampers seemed to be in excellent condition.

This is just my opinion, however, as I know some TR owners prefer the feel of the standard lever arm set up. To this day I have never had to alter the shock absorber from the mid way point that I original set it at.

Hubba Hubba: TR4A Rear Hub Rebuild (same as TR5, TR6, Stag and Triumph 2000 and 2500)

With the new MOT regulations coming into force in May 2018 and with the spectre of some MOT stations not being equipped/capable or even willing to test Classic Cars in the future I thought I would "test" the various options on offer from various Garages/repair shops, so after my TR4A sailed through its mot with no advisories I took it to Lazarus Cars for their 40 point Certificated safety check. The result was that the test detected too much play in the rear N/S wheel bearing. On the bright side it showed that there are ways of getting your Classic Car tested should modern MOT stations advance to a stage where they can't/won't test a Classic car. The down side was that I had to address the issue as although I make glib remarks about the condition of my TR (usually based on looking at pristine examples) I have always kept "the parts that matter" in as good a condition as quality parts availability allow. Some will say that rebuilding the rear hubs is a specialist job but all you really need is a hub puller and a vice although a set of blind bearing pullers make life easier.

Years ago when I was still in work I had had the foresight to have a hub puller made up to fit my TR and the 2000 Saloon that I owned at the time, all I felt that I now needed was a thin 2" AF spanner which I managed to create (the cheapest 2" AF spanner I could find was £60) by grinding a 50mm spanner (you can also make a "spanner" out of ¼" or even 3/16" steel). I also didn't want to have the car off the road so I bought a pair of used hubs from someone who had replaced their hubs and drive shafts with uprated hubs and CV jointed shafts so that I could recondition them and then swap them for the ones on my car. Now a description of the work for those who may need to carry it out on their cars, reconditioning the bought used hubs before removing the old ones which I did a few weeks later -

With the hub assembly held by the UJ yokes in a vice and after removing the nyloc nut and the washer that hold the hub onto the stub axle I put the protective "cap" on the end of the axle to protect the thread and placed my hub puller on the drive flange using nuts to bolt it to the wheel studs, I then realised that the amount of torque that would be needed to draw the flange off the keyed and tapered axle would very likely damage or distort the UJ yoke so I marked out the positions of the holes in the hub flange that give access to the nuts that hold the hub to the radius arm onto the hub puller, removed the puller then drilled holes (only needed the one in the end) in the hub puller to allow me to bolt a 3ft piece of angle iron.

The hub puller was then re fitted to the drive flange. The angle iron when pulled in the opposite rotation of the power bar turning the hub puller bolt locked against the hub so that no strain was put on the yoke. I was able to hold the angle iron while tightening the hub puller bolt and the flange soon parted from the axle with a loud "crack", Hubtastic! I said.

The hub bearing housing was then lifted off to leave the inner bearing and collapsible spacer on the axle. It was straight forward then to remove the outer bearing races and seals from the hub using a parallel punch in the recesses machined in the hub for this purpose.

After using a pipe grip to remove the collapsible spacer I had to use a "blind" bearing puller to draw the inner bearing off the axle and also the bearing off the wheel flange, then with the stone guard and adjusting spacer removed the locking tabs on the 2 large float adjusting nuts (2inch AF) were flattened and the 2 nuts were removed.

ANGLE IRON

The whole assembly was now down to its components parts.

The new bearing outer races were then pressed into the hub using the old ones which I cut with a thin cutting disc to allow them to "spring" and not get stuck in the hub and the new tapered bearing was installed using a large socket and vice to press the one bearing onto the drive flange. After cleaning up the threads on the axle and 2" AF nuts they were given a liberal coating of copper grease and along with a new locking washer were fitted to the axle with the adjusting spacer and stone guard, the new bearing was then placed on the tapered axle and very gently tapped into place using a piece of steel pipe over the axle (as long as the pipe locates on the steel inner race and you ensure it is square you won't damage the bearing).

After giving all the bearings a good greasing a new collapsible spacer was fitted and the hub was put in place. Next came the fitting of the key and the wheel flange which were then fixed in place with the washer and a new nyloc nut.

The next stage takes a bit of patience as the end float has to be adjusted via the thicker 2" AF nut, unlike front wheel tapered bearings which you can tighten up then "back off" the adjusting nut, if you over tighten the rear hubs it means that the collapsible spacer must be replaced so the drive flange has to come back off. The best way to do this is to use a DTI (Dial Test Indicator) more commonly known as a clock gauge to obtain the correct end float of 0.003", but, some people are experienced enough to hold the assembly in a vice and lever the flange until there is minimal movement (any movement at the flange will by multiplied when the road wheel is fitted and pulled to feel that movement).

With the other hub reconditioned fast forward to removing the old hubs and fitting the reconditioned ones.

Starting with the N/S rear, the car was jacked up and placed on 2 axle stands and the road wheel removed, handbrake cable disconnected and brake drum removed. Using a ½" AF socket

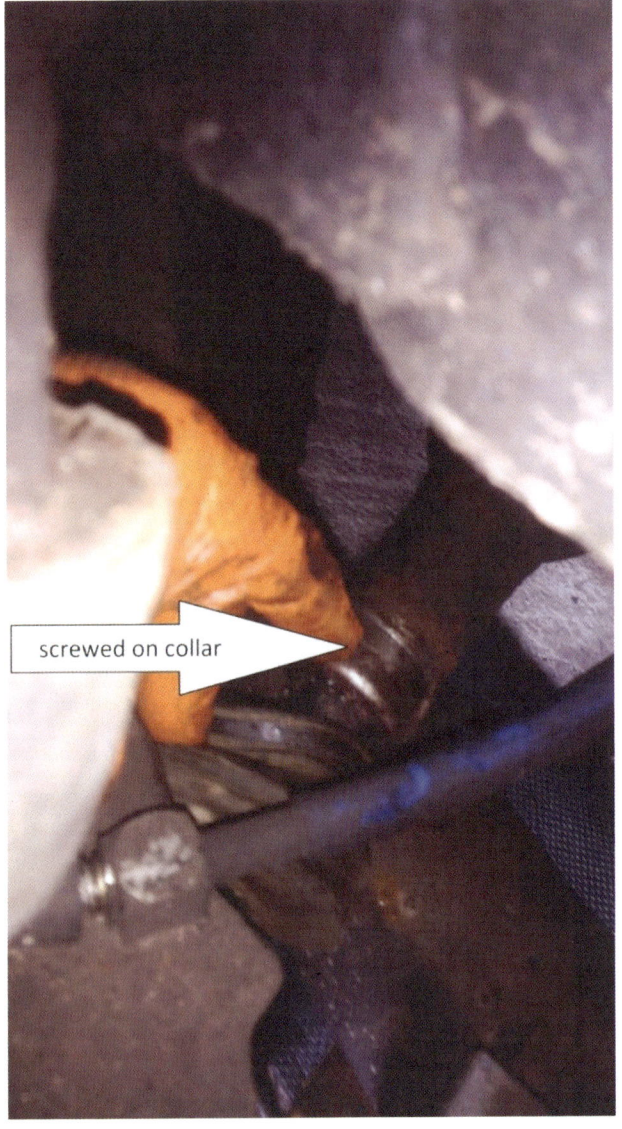

screwed on collar

the 6 X 5/16" UNF Nyloc nuts that hold the hub to the radius arm were removed, the wheel flange has holes in it which allow access to these nuts.

The tie wraps holding the gaiter onto the drive shaft were then snipped off and the collar which helps prevent the outer drive shaft from coming away from the inner shaft was unscrewed.

The outer driveshaft can then be drawn out of the radius arm if you just move the brake shoe return springs out of the way slightly (unfortunately on Stag's, 2000's, 2500's and 2.5 PI's the brake shoes and handbrake system have to be removed as it's a different set up), but as I wanted to clean up all the brake parts I removed the shoes at this point although I left the wheel cylinder attached to the brake back plate to save me from having to bleed the brakes.

With the brakes all cleaned up using brake cleaning fluid I removed the brake shoe adjuster, stripped it down and used copper grease to re assemble it. After I removed the original hub from the outer driveshaft the reconditioned hub assembly was fitted to it using a new Universal Joint. With the splines well greased the outer driveshaft along with its gaiter were carefully re installed along with the brake components and adjusted accordingly.

It was then the turn for the O/S.

With the reconditioned hubs fitted it was time for a test drive, the car went as smoothly as before (possibly smoother, but that may have been my imagination) and I know that these hubs will now last longer than me, so what to do with the spare hubs? Well with time on my hands I stripped these down and fitted new bearings, seals etc so that I could pass them on to someone else.

Trunnion Lubrication: An Alternative?

Over the years I have read many articles about the correct lubrication for the lower trunnions on our Triumphs and I don't think that many will argue that SAE 90 or similar is the recommended lubricant. Some people get very aggravated when the term "grease your trunnions" is used as they will quite rightly point out that over time the grease gets hard and inhibits the addition of fresh grease through the nipple. The advocates of grease will say that if you grease them regularly and use a high pressure pump the old grease will be displaced before it goes hard and that grease will adhere better to the vertical link and lower trunnion "threads", also true.

There is of course a third option. While I was still in employment as an Engineering Operations Manager in the Tobacco industry I was responsible for all machinery in the factory. A lot of the packing machinery was made in Italy, they were state of the art, but like a lot of Italian prototype machinery some of the tolerances were shall we say on the generous side and this led to premature oil seal failures and the resultant leaks. As any risk of product contamination was totally unacceptable these machines had to have their oil seals changed every month which meant four days downtime with two technicians working on them which was not only a drain on my budget, but also meant that production had to be made up by costly overtime.

I commissioned the help of a Formula 1 racing lubrication guru who had been carrying out some research on all kinds of lubrication over a previous ten year period and he recommended that I procured some Shell Retinax TL 00 semi fluid grease which I did and the next time that seals on a machine started to weep the oil was drained from the modules and the semi fluid grease was used instead of oil, the seals were not changed. This was repeated on all the other packing machines when they started to weep oil.

After 12 months there had been no sign of oil weeps/leaks on any of the machines so the first machine that had semi fluid grease added instead of oil was stripped down and there was no sign of wear on any of the internal parts and the grease was as fluid as the day it was added. The internal components in these modules were made up of bearings, bushes, sliding shafts, gears and just about any type of moving part that you could think of and manufactured from just about any material. Ever since then I have used Shell Retinax TL00 in the Trunnions on my TR4A, my Herald 13/60 and my Vignale and when I pump new semi fluid grease it flows in well and pushes the old grease out through the top dust seal (though I do warm the grease first). I recently had to remove one trunnion from my TR4A as there was play in the pivot bolt and I inspected the trunnion, there was no sign of wear.

I'm not saying that you should use semi fluid grease, but it gives you an option should you be undecided about what to use. My opinion is that since our cars were originally manufactured there have been many advances and improvements in the materials and parts that are available to us (eg electronic ignition) and that Triumph engineers may well have opted for the type of semi fluid grease that is available today for the trunnions if it had been available at the time, perhaps they experimented with what was available back then and it wasn't acceptable, I don't know, I just know what works in my cars. I have also used this grease in noisy differentials and it can make a massive difference, extending the life of a worn differential sometimes for many years.

TR4A Lower Trunnion Repair.

When I had my TR4A MOT'd the tester, Martin, gave me an advisory for slight wear in the lower N/S trunnion bushes. I was a bit concerned that it might be the actual brass trunnion itself as I had installed poly bushes only a couple of years ago and I did not want to buy a new trunnion as I have had a few reports and messages about the poor quality of the available brass trunnions the main issue being that some are a poor fit on the vertical links. When I got the car home I immediately jacked the car up and placed it on axle stands but no matter how much leverage I applied I could not find any movement. Most people would probably have left it at that and put it down to the tester not knowing classic cars that well, but my problem was that Martin is an excellent tester and knows classic cars extremely well. I had to investigate further.

I removed the road wheel and the split pin and castle nut that keeps the trunnion pivot bolt in place and with my trolley jack supporting the lower wishbones until the pivot bolt turned quite freely I used a brass dolly to drift the pivot bolt out and then swivelled the hub upwards and wedged a block of wood between it and the road spring to make examination possible. I examined the bushes and they were as good as new with no sign of any play when I replaced the pivot bolt into the lower wishbones (those who do not know the TR4 – 6 trunnion set up please note that the bushes and sleeves locate in the lower wishbones and not in the trunnion bore as on Spitfires and Herald's etc). I used a micrometer to measure the diameter of the bolt and the part that locates in the brass trunnion was worn a few thousandths of an inch. I placed the pivot bolt in the brass trunnion and I could feel very slight play, but more than the few thou of pivot bolt ware would have given, therefore the hole in the trunnion was also worn. Martin had been correct and if my TR4A was mot exempt at the time, would I have taken it for a voluntary mot ? I'd like to think so, but I know of a few people who are not taking their cars for an mot now that they don't legally have to, just think what faults they may be over looking and although this trunnion fault was not dangerous at this stage, it might well have progressed without me noticing it. I removed the front hub by removing the wheel grease cap and removing the split pin and wheel bearing nut, this enabled me to unscrew the brass trunnion from the vertical link.

As I wrote earlier, I have heard that there are poor quality replacements on the market and the threads on my trunnion and the vertical link felt like new so I did not want to change the trunnion. Being a former toolmaker I still have a selection of expandable reamers, so using these I slowly increased the diameter of the hole in the trunnion until I achieved a light drive fit for the same size sleeve that is used in the poly bushes that locate in the lower wishbones. I did not attempt to drill the hole larger as brass tends to "snatch" on drill bits, especially when you are enlarging an existing hole or one that is oval through wear.

With the sleeve cut to the length of the trunnion I inserted the pivot bolt and I could not feel any play, however, as I had purchased a new pivot bolt I used that and it was a very nice sliding fit in the now sleeved trunnion.

I then 3/4 filled the trunnion with semi fluid grease (I find this easier to do when it's apart than pumping any form of lubricant in after assembly) and screwed the trunnion onto the vertical link with a rag underneath to catch the excess lubricant as it overflowed, replaced the wheel hub, adjusted the wheel bearing (with added new grease) and attached the trunnion to the lower wishbones with a liberal coating of grease.

Job done and a good saving on the price of a trunnion.

SECTION 7 Body Work

Door Cards for Most Models

Shortly after I bought my TR4A I purchased a pair of door cards from a well-known supplier, The quality wasn't that great and a few years later I had a set made up by an upholsterer that were far better but still not worth the cost.

When I retired I took an upholstery course and learnt how to make car seat covers, but it was so laborious that I vowed to only ever make covers if there were none available to buy, no matter what the cost! However, the other day I decided that I would make a set of door cards for my TR4A and incorporate an elasticated pocket in each one for my "bits and bobs". As I had learnt how to make traditional piping on the course I also decided to edge the door cards and the pocket with white piping to match my seats.

Cheap plastic piping on the left with my home-made piping on the right.

If you have tatty door cards, but with good wooden backing that fits well you could re use them, just strip off the vinyl, but I wanted to keep my old cards to sell on as they were in excellent condition.

I bought a sheet of 3mm millboard (hardboard) and after removing the old door cards I cut the shape of one door card and after measuring where the trim clip and other holes should be I drilled them to their respective sizes, I then cut a slot for the pocket.

Next I cut the vinyl 50mm oversize on all edges and cut a piece of vinyl for the pockets. I cut 4 oz Dacron (you can use thin foam) to the shape of the board and glued (using upholstery adhesive) the Dacron central to the vinyl covers. When the glue dried I used the same adhesive to glue a light cloth (cotton flock backing paper, but most thin papers can be used) onto the

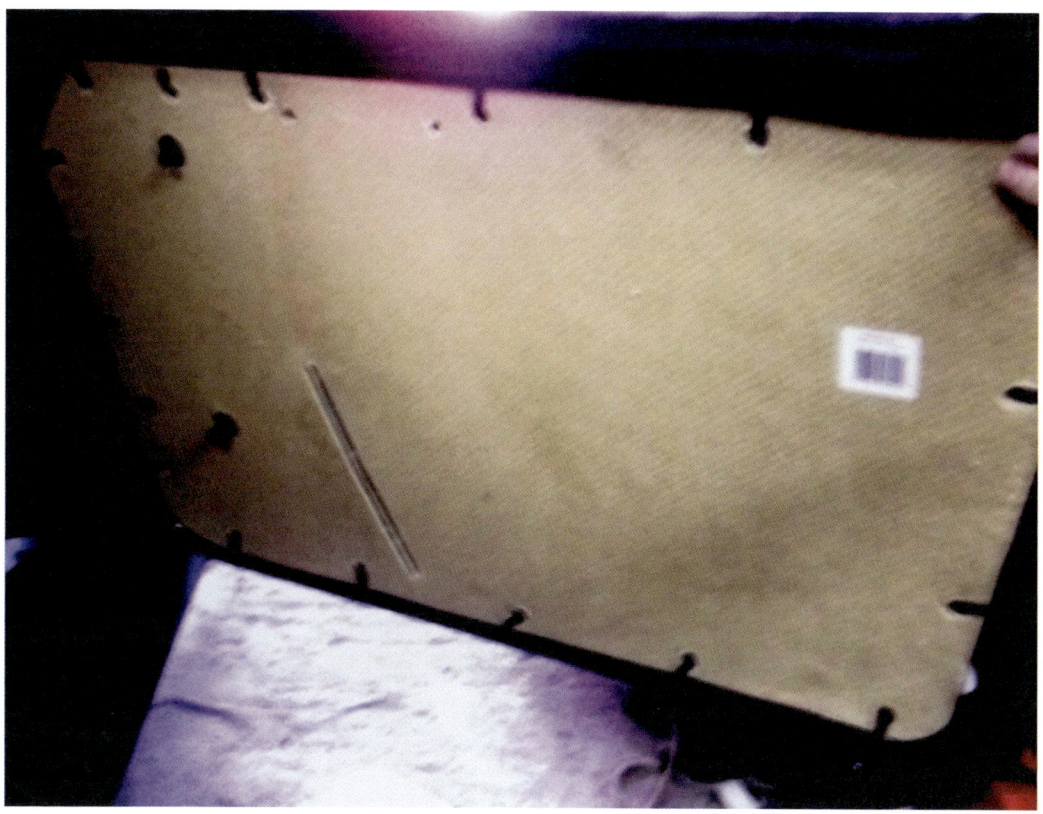

Dacron, then after marking four straight lines along the width of the vinyl I used my sewing machine to create four straight(ish) stitch lines.

I then made the pockets up with 20mm wide elastic in the top "hem" and the bottom of the pocket sewn to the door card vinyl then folded over it so that the bottom stitch line was not visible when the pocket was in its final position.

The vinyl cover (including the rear vertical fold of the pocket) was then stretched over the hardboard edges and stapled from the back using 4mm staples, long enough to do the job, but not long enough to protrude through the vinyl cover.

Next the front vertical/angled fold of the pocket was pulled through the slot in the board and stapled in position. Both ends of the elastic were stapled to the board to give the required tension for the elasticated pocket top. Hole punches were used through the holes in the board to make the handle pull, window winder and door handle holes in the vinyl.

Next I had to make the piping, you can buy rolls of plastic extrusion, but it does not look anywhere as near as good as traditional handmade piping, so after cutting up strips of white vinyl, stitching them together to make a strip long enough to go right around the edges of the two door cards and pockets, then folding in the rope, I used my piping attachment on my sewing machine to create about 8 metres of piping with a 12mm "land" for stapling or gluing in position. This was then stapled to the back of the hardboard for the edging and glued in place for the pockets.

You can make your minds up about how good/bad they look but, believe me, they are far better than the ones that I bought and were only a fraction of the cost. It's also surprising at what a difference nice door cards make to the interior of your car and of course the method that I used here can be used on most cars, not just TR4As.

TR4A Driver Door Window Problem

While driving my TR4A on a run September 2016 I incurred a problem with the window in the driver's door. A few times when I attempted to wind the window back up it "stuck" momentarily and then released with a "click". Unusually for me I decided to have a look for the cause the very next day instead of leaving it and hoping that it would cure itself (a method which has sometimes stood me in good stead over my years of TR ownership). After removing the door pull handle, window winder and latch handle I unclipped the door card and removed the plastic membrane. After close inspection with a small mirror and lamp (the fault wouldn't occur to help me find it, typical) I found that the front (almost) vertical window guide had become detached from its lower fixing bracket. With this removed it was a simple job to re rivet the bracket onto the bracket, at last a simple fix on my TR which has saved me from breaking my window.

THESE 2 PARTS HAVE COME ADRIFT DUE TO BROKEN RIVETS

TR4A Rear Lower Wing Repair

I had noticed a couple of years ago that the bottom of my rear wings where they meet the sill were starting to corrode, not surprising as the car is used all the year round. I sprayed various maintenance fluids over the corrosion and in between the wings and sill ends every few months as I know from experience that when you start cutting out rust you nearly always find more than you thought that there would be and your car can be off the road for a while, I am also planning to restore the car at some point, but I can't bring myself to take it off the road to do so, and I was hoping that the wings would last until that day arrived (if it ever does).

Anyway, with work needed on my rear N/S hub and my Herald 13/60 needing more road and less garage time I decided that I would at least address the rot in the wings.

With the car jacked up and placed on axle stands I started cutting out the bottom of the wings to see how bad the corrosion was. To be honest it wasn't half as bad as I thought it would be as on both sides the bottom of the inner wheel arch were solid and although both the sill ends were holed, the repairs to the sills would be hidden behind the wing repair patches.

Using my angle grinder I made the cut outs as neat as possible then tidied everything up with my Dremel.

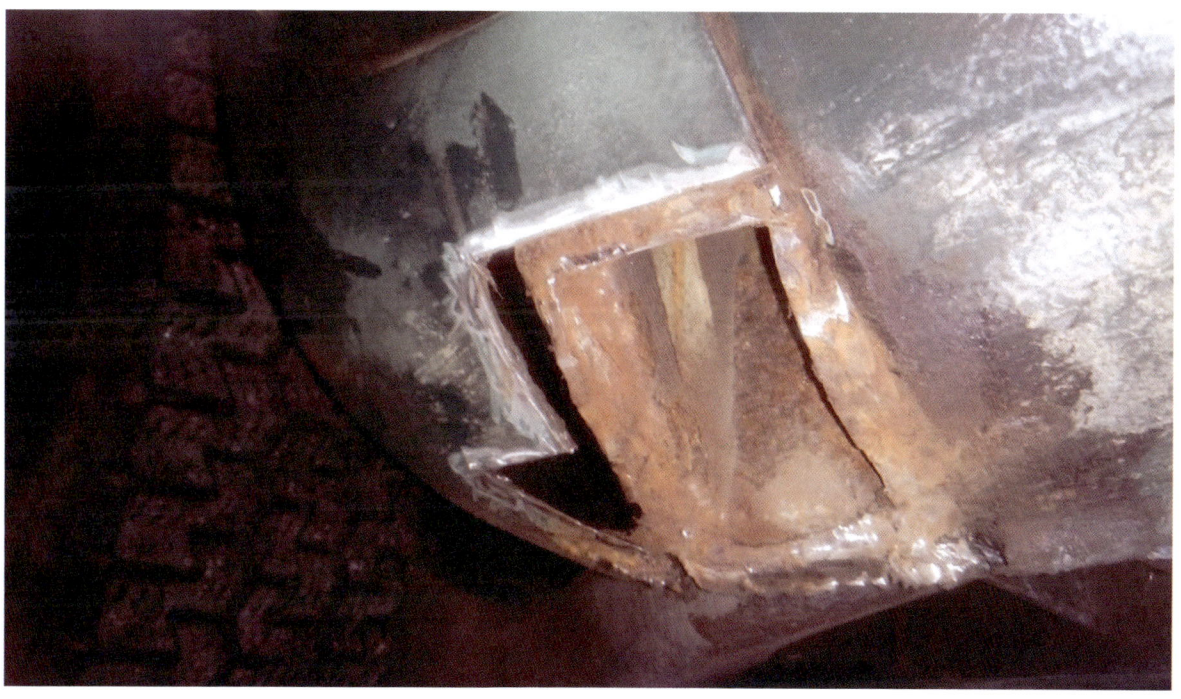

Next I gave all the surface rust 3 coats of rust converter. Cardboard patterns were then made for the sill end repairs and the shape was then transferred onto 1.2mm thick sheet steel as the sills are structural. With the metal repair patches cut out they were painted both sides with zinc weld through primer and seam welded in place.

As these repairs would be hidden I didn't bother grinding the welds down, they were just painted with etch primer and more weld through primer.

Cardboard patterns were then made to the shape of the wing repairs and transferred to 1mm thick sheet steel with holes punched into the bottom lip so that they could be plug welded to the sills. These were then painted with zinc weld through primer and seam welded in place. Before the bottom lips were plug welded I pulled the wing bottoms away from the sills and sprayed rust inhibitor between the wings and sill ends.

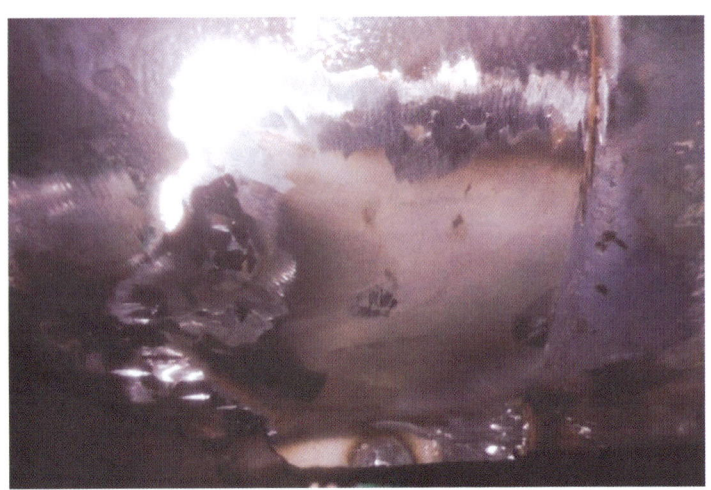

After grinding back the welds the repaired areas were given a coat of acid etch primer, then primed,

filled and stoppered before the final "flat back", then 3 coats of primer were applied, flatted back and then 5 light coats of cellulose Fern Green were applied. When the paint was fully hardened the painted areas were flatted back with 1200wet or dry then polished with cutting compound. I can't say that it is a perfect colour match, however, as the repair is on the bottom curvature of

the wing and the paint has been blended out along the sill you have to lie on the floor to see the difference! The bonnet , front scuttle and windscreen frame are Brooklands Green, maybe one day it will be the same colour all over, but the important thing for me is that the sills are now structurally sound and the bottom of the wings have no rust and look good. I then sprayed rust inhibiting wax into the sill from inside the car as well as into the gap between the wing bottom and sill and the rear of the wing. Hopefully this means that the dreaded restoration date can be set back another few years!

Whether two rust holes or four a TR is more!

Surrey Top Project July 2013

I had always admired the TR's with Surrey tops fitted (for those unfamiliar with them they consist of a frame with a glass or Perspex/makrolon window which is fixed to the rear deck, you then have the option of either a "hard top" or a "soft top" roof insert), I think that they compliment the lines of any TR4 -6 but that is only my opinion. I had never *really* wanted one as I like the ease with which a TR soft top can be folded back and the cost of one had always been too much for me to spend on a "whim".

However, I wanted to find out whether one was right for me or not so the only thing to do was to bite the bullet and buy one as I didn't know anybody personally who has one fitted and in any case something like this can take a while to assess, using it in different weather and on long trips etc.

My plan was to buy a second hand one then sell it on for the same price if I didn't like it. As usual my plan was flawed. After months searching auction sites the only "genuine" Surrey tops that came up were for the backlight part only and they all sold for around the £1800 mark plus the fuel it would cost to pick them up. I am not even sure if all of these were genuine or reproduction backlights as sometimes the sellers were "very vague".

I contacted the 2 large Triumph Parts suppliers and was pleasantly surprised by the outcome, 1 could supply all the parts I required, but not from Stock and the one backlight they had was a returned item. The other supplier had all the items in stock and for less than £835 including delivery (for the soft top roof insert and the Perspex backlight window option) they arrived two days after I placed the order, great service.

I had heard many horror stories of poorly made and ill fitting aftermarket backlight/Surrey tops, so I thought that I would leave it until the winter months before I attempted to fit it.

The next day found me in the garage removing the soft top and frame, there were no instructions on how to fit the Surrey Top, but being a man I wouldn't have read them anyway so I wasn't perturbed. The first anomaly I spotted was that there were 7 studs protruding from the backlight frame and there were only 5 holes (for the rear of the soft top to bolt onto) on my TR4A. I fitted the backlight assembly in position and was able to position the 2 surplus studs just inside the edge of the cockpit. I then loosely assembled the soft top insert frame along with the soft top insert, but could not work out how it fitted to the windscreen frame. After half an hour on the internet I worked out that I needed a TR4 type aluminium windscreen frame capping as it has provision for two snap poppers and an extended lip at the front for the soft top roof to tuck into. I should have looked more closely at Surrey tops in the past as I am not happy that this is a well thought out way of fixing a roof, but there must be thousands of TR's with this arrangement so I rang the supplier and ordered one (another £73). While looking for information about fitting the roof section I read that some people used the front of a Spitfire frame along with the handles, so I may look at that option if I'm not happy with the standard set up. I want to be able to quickly remove the roof and store it behind the seats which the standard set up allows, this will enable me to carry more equipment for runs than I currently can with the soft top hood frame lowered. I decided that I would re fit my original soft top and frame and wait until after examining the TR's with Surrey tops fitted at the TR show in Malvern before I installed my Surrey top. This took me about 2 hours.

The next day I removed the Perspex window and painted the backlight frame (about 4 hours including time between coats of paint) the same colour that I had recently painted my bonnet

(BRG) as eventually the whole car will be painted that colour (it currently has a few different shades of green) with the view to storing it until the winter, then predictably the next day found me re fitting the window and installing the backlight on my car (after first of all cutting off the two "surplus" studs).

I wasn't at all happy with the lack of rigidity of the front of the backlight and I had to cut about 2mm off the front lip of the backlight where it rested on the B post to get a nice line along the door windows. To resolve the rigidity issue I made two brackets out of 1.5mm sheet steel that I was able to slide up into the hollow ridge of the backlight and with two 5mm nuts welded to the plate I was able to sandwich the lip of the backlight between the brackets and two other steel plates. I utilised the soft top frame fixing holes to secure the brackets to the car. Another four hours work to get to this stage. Friday, and two days after I had ordered the windscreen capping it hadn't arrived and I wanted to use the TR for a S. Wales Area run on Sunday, I called the supplier and they said they had just posted it and I would not receive it until Monday, I wasn't happy, but I decided to keep the backlight on and hope that there was not too much rain on the day of the run.

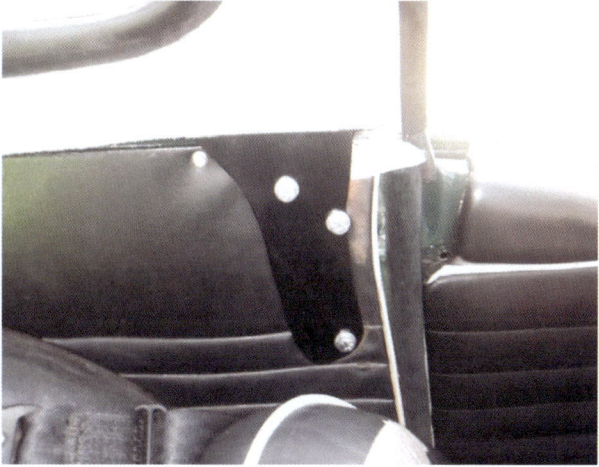

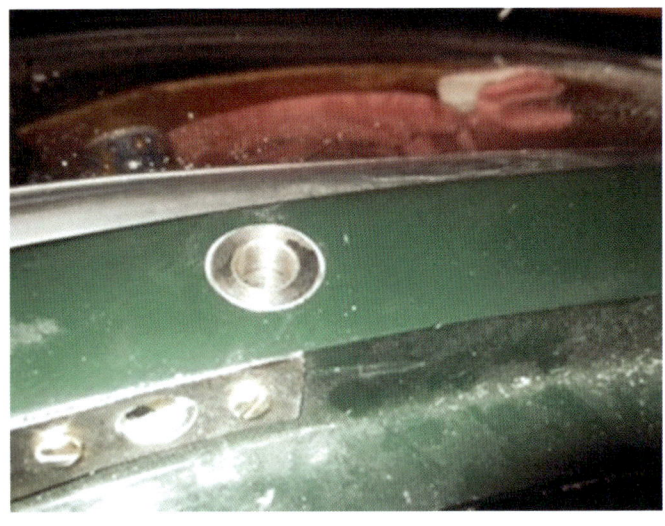

I took the TR for a blast down a private road near me and with the speedo needle nudging 105mph the back light felt reasonably firm.

Sunday, with the good weather continuing, thankfully I had no need for the soft top roof insert (this is the part that is actually the Surrey Top) and I was pleasantly surprised at how "open" the car felt with the backlight fitted, also my stereo speakers were not covered by a folded down soft top and the amount of air turbulence at speed was greatly reduced. Over 150 miles in glorious sunshine and I was very happy with the conversion.

Monday, the finisher arrived late afternoon and I riveted it in place, I had to lever the extended lip up to make a gap large enough for the lip of the Surrey Top to fit in, I left it over night to let the top stretch in readiness for the snap poppers to be fitted. About half an hour spent doing this.

Tuesday arrived and with the car outside in the sun to allow me to be able to pull the top nice and taught to fit the poppers in position so that the top was "crease free" I turned my attention to the holes in the backlight where the top frame locates. To prevent unsightly scratch marks I made a couple of stainless steel plates to cover the area and screwed them in position. Then I spent the next couple of hours fitting the poppers to the front finisher, top of the backlight frame and finally in the Surrey top itself, removing the top after each popper position had been marked to rivet the two halves of the popper together using the correct tool. To make the holes in the Surrey top I heated the shank of a 4mm drill and pushed it through the vinyl (this prevents the vinyl from fraying). All in all this took me about 2 ½ hours.

With the Surrey top in place I took the TR for a trial run and at 60mph the front of the Surrey top came out of the finisher! It was lucky that my son Jack was with me to hold it down! I pulled into a lay bye and re inserted the front of the Surrey top and started off for home, I took the car up to the speed limit of 70mph and the top stayed in place! Could the combined speed of 60mph + head wind have caused it to come out? I have heard of this happening but at much higher speeds. I intended to give it another trial and I hoped to take the TR to the Barry Waterfront show in five days time on July 28th(it depended on if my daughter wanted to accompany me and Jack, if so I would have to take my 13/60). After that I wasn't going to get another chance to use the TR until the TR international on August 11th due to holidays. I wasn't happy, with two good runs coming up (TR international and TSSC family weekend) I had to either resolve the issue or re fit the hood.

I managed to take the TR out twice before the Barry Waterfront show and using a private road near my house I took the car up to 80mph, both times the Surrey top stayed in place, I was pretty sure that there was nothing different to the way that I had inserted the leading edge of the Surrey top into the finisher at the time that it had detached itself as it only slots under the finisher, but that's TR's for you. My daughter and her friend decided to accompany us to the Barry Waterfront show, but a friend offered them a lift which meant that I could give the TR a test run, also the

weather forecast for the day of the show was heavy rain showers so the top would get a good try out.

With a sustained speed of 70mph on the M4 the Surrey top stayed in place, also even though there was only light rain, it proved to be at least as water tight as the fold down hood.

So, what are my conclusions at this early stage –

1) The quality of the parts provided was far better than I had expected after reading other people's write ups.
2) The value for money when compared with a second hand original unit is excellent.
3) Ease of fitting was far easier than other write ups I had seen indicated.
4) The lines of the car look much cleaner with the backlight and Surrey top.
5) The interior of the car feels more "roomier" than before and is a better place to be in.
6) Would I recommend an aftermarket Surrey Top conversion to other TR owners – YES.

After using the TR with the Surrey top for the TR International and TSSC Stafford weekend I was very happy with it, although both weekends had very good weather and the top was off for all the runs. While at the TR international I examined the TR's with Surrey tops and found that in the main (but not all) they had the poppers on the front of the windscreen frame capping either screwed or riveted to the windscreen frame, I removed the front poppers on mine, bent the capping down onto the frame and used self tapping screws to replicate this. I also made a couple of top hat bushes out of stainless steel and drilled out the holes on the top of the backlight frame where the Surrey top rear bar locates (and is held with the thumb screws) to accommodate the bushes. This modification makes it easier to locate the bar and decreases the chances of scratching the paint on the backlight frame.

Footnote:

It is now 6 years since I have fitted the Surrey top and I have no plans to revert to the soft top. The car is used throughout the winter and the top still remains as weather resistant as the soft top. I am extremely pleased.

Bonnet Respray

My TR4 when I bought it was a Jaguar Fern Green colour, quite nice, but a bit "weak" for my liking. Quite a few years ago I repaired the driver's door and at the time I couldn't get quite the right colour match so I painted the front wing and rear wing the same colour so that you had to look very carefully to see the colour miss match.

Previously I had repaired the windscreen surround and decided that I would gradually turn the car Brooklands Racing Green which is actually closer to the colour that I painted the O/S door and wings so I painted the windscreen surround and front scuttle in BRG, which then contrasted greatly with the bonnet as they were on the same plane.

As I had finally (hopefully) sorted the engine miss fire I now had the time to paint the bonnet BRG so that the car would only be two different colours. Here is an account of how I went about it, professional or competent paint prayers please look away, but as I have said in the past my

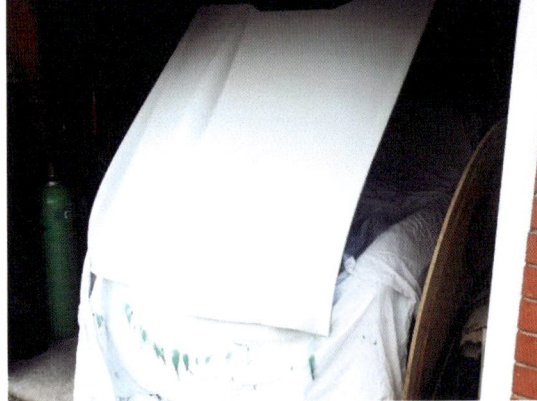

methods work for me and anyone who needs to freshen up their Triumph's paint or even re spray the whole car can achieve an excellent finish by following my method without the need to pay for a professional paint job.

Monday 24th June

After removing the Triumph letters and Globe badge I gave the bonnet a quick clean then wet sanded it back with 360 wet or dry paper, rubbing along the length of the bonnet. I then sanded the edges of the bonnet and flatted out the marks that the bonnet had acquired over the years.

With some cellulose thinners on a rag I tested to see if the existing paint reacted with the cellulose thinners, it didn't which hopefully meant that I could use cellulose primer straight on the old paint. If there was a reaction I would have to use an isolating paint like Barcoat.

After wiping the bonnet with a tack rag I applied some high build primer (mixed 50/50) to the marks that I had flatted out then after about ten minutes I gave the entire bonnet a coat of high build primer. After another ten minutes I applied another coat, then a final coat ten minutes after that. I intended to leave it like this for 24 – 48 hours before flatting back before top coating.

This took less than 2 hours

Tuesday 25th June

Well as usual I didn't have the patience to wait 48 hours so after sanding the whole bonnet down with wet 600 wet or dry paper (taking great care not to break though the primer on the raised edges), drying it with a cloth then wiping the bonnet with a clean tack rag I first applied a coat of BRG (70% thinners 30% paint) to the edges of the bonnet and then a dust coat of BRG all over the bonnet After about 15 minutes I again sprayed the edges of the bonnet then applied a coat to the bonnet. I left this for 20 minutes then applied another coat of BRG. After another 20 minutes I applied another coat of BRG and repeated this until I had applied a total of (including the dust coat) 9 coats of BRG. This was a bit excessive, but I was using my new 6ooml gravity fed gun and it was taking a bit of getting used to, the finish was nice and shiny but it had a bit of an orange peel finish that I would need to polish out, hence the extra coats of paint and the beauty of cellulose paint.

This took a total of 4 hours and 36 cups of coffee to fill in the drying time between coats of paint.

Tuesday 24th July

Well I managed to keep my hands off the bonnet for a month, so today I wet flatted the bonnet using 1200 grit paper, then I cut it back using G3 rubbing compound. The bonnet came up with a nice shine (I could get better if I had the patience to T cut it, but polishing bores me rigid, so perhaps I'll go over it again in the future). Next I re installed the Triumph Globe badge and letters. This took about 2 hours the longest part of the job was fitting the new plastic badge grommets.

So all in all it only took about eight hours to paint and cut back the bonnet, but it took a month when allowing for paint hardening time, this can be reduced if you don't use a rubbing compound and concentrate on achieving a better finish straight from the spray gun (which is what I will do the next time I paint a panel). The materials cost about £40 and there is enough paint and thinners to paint another three panels on the car.

If you decide to have a go yourself just remember a few things,

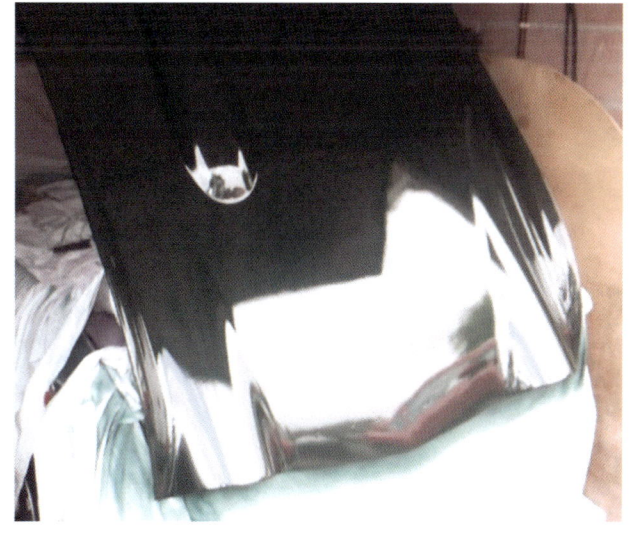

1) The area is well ventilated and you have the correct mask and filter.

2) Check to see if the paint on the panel you are going to spray will not react with cellulose paint, if it does, either take it back to bare metal, then etch prime it before applying primer or use an isolating coat such as Barcoat.

3) Ensure that you have a nice clean and dry air supply for your spray gun.

4) Should you have any runs in the paint, don't panic, let them dry over night then use a sharp craft knife to "shave" the run down then flat it out before applying more coats of paint (or even "shave" it off and flat it back when you have applied all your top coats).

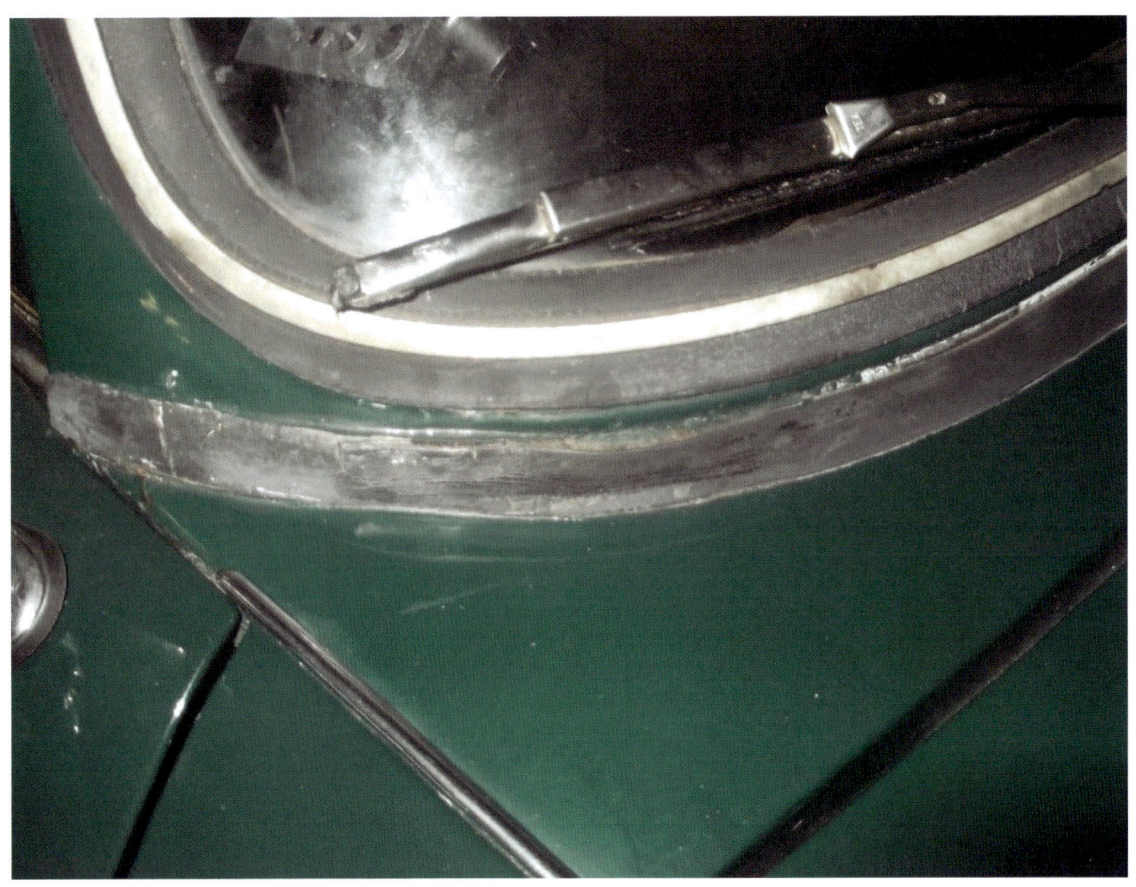

Windscreen Frame Repair October 2012

Although this article concerns the work carried out on my TR4A, it is relevant to all pre MKIV Spitfires, TR4s, TR5s TR250s and TR6s as they all use the removable windscreen frame. They do have different part numbers though as there is a slight difference, the TR frames have captive nuts for the different style hood clasps. I have written a very detailed account of the repairs and I am sure that most of you will skip through paragraphs, but I know that there are some out there who have not yet attempted body work repairs and painting and it is with these people in mind that I have written it this way, to give them the confidence and information that they need to enable them to tackle body work jobs on their cars, and to learn from my mistakes! As I have pointed out before, I am no expert and some professionals will cringe at my methods, but they work for me!

At the start of the year I had noticed that the bottom of the Windscreen frame had a few small rust bubbles on the N/S and I had been putting off the inevitable removal of the frame and addressing the issue until the winter months arrived. I saw a NOS windscreen frame at the TR International at Malvern, but the price was £400 and I would not dream of laying out that kind of money unless mine was totally beyond repair. Most of us have experienced the horror of finding out how badly an area of a car has corroded when we strip back paint to address a small bubble in the paint work and I have changed enough windscreens on old Triumphs to know that there is virtually always a corrosion issue that needs welding when the windscreen and rubber are removed even on the most pristine looking cars, so I was prepared for the worst and I wasn't (or should that be *was* disappointed) when I finally got around to tackling the job. I did take the precaution, however, of procuring a spare frame which was in need of repairs, but was repairable if I found that mine was not (thanks to a friend, who only wanted me to carry out a day's welding on his Spitfire as payment – top man).

After I had removed the carpets from the sides of the foot wells I gave the frame fixing nuts and bolts a good soaking with penetrating fluid. The next job was to remove the windscreen wipers then drill out the pop rivets which hold the aluminium finisher to the top of the frame and carefully separate it from the bead of sealant which still held it in place. Next to be taken off the frame was the rear view mirror and sun visors. With this accomplished I removed the windscreen seal finisher and using a craft knife I carefully cut away the front of the windscreen seal. I never try to re use a seal unless it is impossible to buy a new one, I have seen windscreens crack when someone has tried to push out the screen as our cars are much more than likely to have had some screen sealant or silicone used on them to stop leaks over the years and this bonds the screen to the seal making removal difficult. With the front of the seal removed I noticed that the seal had taken a layer of paint and filler from the "good" lower O/S bottom of the frame revealing aluminium mesh that is used to fill holes in car body work before covering it with filler!! My worst fears realised, the frame was rotten!!

Applying SLIGHT pressure all around and using the craft knife to separate any of the seal that was sticking to the screen I gently eased the screen out and stored it safely. The three clamps were then removed from the base of the frame that secured it to the top of the front scuttle through the dashboard. I then removed the two nuts from either side of the two locating arms of the frame which slot into brackets that are bolted at the back of the A post under the dashboard. With these removed I tried to ease the frame out of its fixings, but it wouldn't budge. I was about to use a "persuader" on it when I had one of those very rare moments in my life when common sense kicked in. "Have a look at your workshop manual" the small part of my brain which still functions told me. So I did and the manual told me that there were two bolts in either side that had to be slackened off before the frame could be removed. These bolts are accessed in the A pillar with the door open. I duly slackened off these bolts (to find that one was missing on the N/S) and with a few slight taps of a rubber mallet the frame came out (mental note: next time I buy a new TV after smashing the old one when ARSENAL fail to win, can't say lose – read the instructions instead of spending the next few weeks frantically pressing buttons on the remote until the TV does what I want).

With the frame placed on a piece of board on top of my TR's boot rack I gently prised away the interior plastic finishing trim leaving the frame totally exposed to reveal the horrific extent of the rot in my frame. The vent flap was then removed from the centre of the scuttle so that I could take it to the paint suppliers for colour matching, my TR is already 3 different shades of green so I didn't want a fourth, I was surprised when I was handed the tin of paint and the colour was quoted as "Truck Green". I really prefer the colour that is on the off side of my car, on the front and rear

wings and the driver door, in retrospect I should have driven the car to the motor factors before I started the job and had that colour matched, I decided though, that when spring arrived I would do this and repaint the frame, scuttle and the bonnet in that shade of green, we'll see!

2 hours

Before cutting away too much metal I had to ensure that I strengthened the frame without losing its shape, so starting at the worse area to enable me to take measurements from the "good" side, I cleaned the edges of the bottom of the frame back to bare metal (where there still was metal !) and made a cardboard template. I marked around the template onto a sheet of steel and reproduced the shape. After using various bits of scrap steel as dollies to obtain as near the correct form as possible (after all it will not be visible) I gave the hidden face a coat of weld through primer *(a point to make here, I had been welding a friends Spitfire and he had supplied the weld through primer, The welds that I produced using that primer were not as "clean" as I would have liked, the arc was effected by the primer, I checked it and it was a mix of 25%aluminium and 75%zinc, the weld through primer that I buy is 99% zinc and gives a good clean splatter less weld)*and welded it into position, using measurements from the other side of the frame to ensure that the dimensions from the top of the frame to the bottom were correct. Another patch was made for the side of the frame (still working on the O/S) painted it as well as the inside of the frame that would be sealed off with weld through primer and welded it in position. At least now there was plenty of strength in this area.

B.J Tip – coat one side of the sheet metal that you are cutting the repair patches from with weld through primer. It is easier to see the scribed lines if you mark out on that side and the steel already has corrosion protection (use the coated side for the areas that you cannot access when the patch is welded in position.

2.5 hours

I had to repair the front of the O/S lower part of the frame by making two patches as there were too many convex and concave curves for my limited talents (and patience) to form on one patch. Next to repair was the outer edge of the frame (still working on the same corner) and the lip that the windscreen seal fits over. These were again made using cardboard templates as patterns

. Some of these repair patches had to have curves and profiles formed into them which was very time consuming. I had to use a hand held mini grinder with a small cut off disc in it to remove some of the more inaccessible corroded steel.

B.J Tip – If you cannot get access to cut or grind off one side of flanged seam (for example the lip that the windscreen seal fits over) "feather" the edge of the patch to match a "feathered" edge on the part that you are going to attach it to.

4 hours

An hour spent with my angle grinder, then my mini grinder with various different grinding wheels and abrasive heads enabled me to smooth down the welds and blend the various joints, after a coat of etch primer I gave the front of the repair a skim of body filler then started to make the cardboard patterns needed for the repairs to the N/S bottom of the frame.

B.J. Tip – If you can afford to pay somebody to do this work for you and still have money left over for the pub, I recommend you do so.

As the lower corner of the N/S of the frame was not nearly as bad as the O/S, the main patch

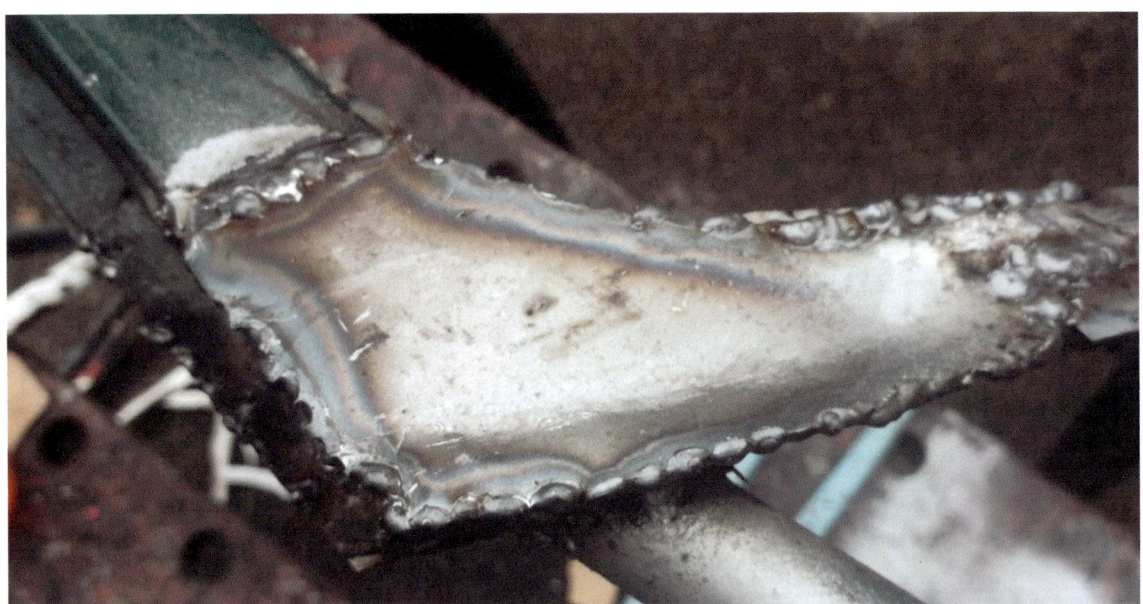

needed was the one for the bottom edge, so after cutting out the corroded steel and inverting the pattern that I had made for the O/S, I scribed around it onto my sheet of steel, cut it out and after coating the inside of the frame and the repair patch with weld through primer I welded it in place. Patterns were then made for the side of the frame and the front. For the front I was able to just about retain the form of the frame along the crease that becomes the lower lip that locates in the rubber moulding which is sandwiched between the scuttle and the frame. With the corroded steel cut away and the inside of the frame coated with weld through primer, I cut out the repair patches, coated them with weld through primer and welded them into position.

2.5 hours

B.J. Tip – if your eye sight is as poor as mine or you are working in bad light, lay your cardboard template/pattern on the side of your sheet steel that you haven't coated with weld through primer and spray over the template/pattern, when you take the template/pattern away you will have a nice clear paint edge to make your cut.

Next I cut out the rusty areas in the side and rear of the N/S lower corner of the frame and made more steel patches, once again coating them with weld through primer before welding them into place. The welds were all then dressed back with my angle grinder and given a coat of etch primer to protect them from future corrosion. After the primer dried I applied a skim of filler and left it to harden.

1 hour

I sanded the filled areas smooth and then sanded back the whole frame using 360 grit wet or dry paper. With my hot air gun in one hand I warmed the frame slightly (as I was doing this outside in October) and then gave the frame four coats of primer from an aerosol can.

1 hour

Leaving the primer to fully harden overnight I sanded it back using 400 grade wet or dry with water, then applied stopper to a few of the small imperfections that were evident. When the stopper had dried I sanded it back again using 400 grade wet or dry and water, wiped the frame with panel wipe and then gave it two coats of cellulose primer using my gravity fed spray gun, again outside, but the weather was quite warm (for October) so I did not need to use my hot air gun to help the paint dry).

.1 hour

The next item to address was the rot on the front scuttle around the aperture where the off side windscreen frame passes through. After first carefully grinding away all the rot with my small hand held grinder I made a cardboard pattern using the near side aperture as a guide, then replicated it on to a piece of sheet steel, after coating it with weld through primer I welded it in place, ground down the welds and applied a thin skim of filler, when this hardened, I sanded it back and applied a skim of stopper.

1 hour

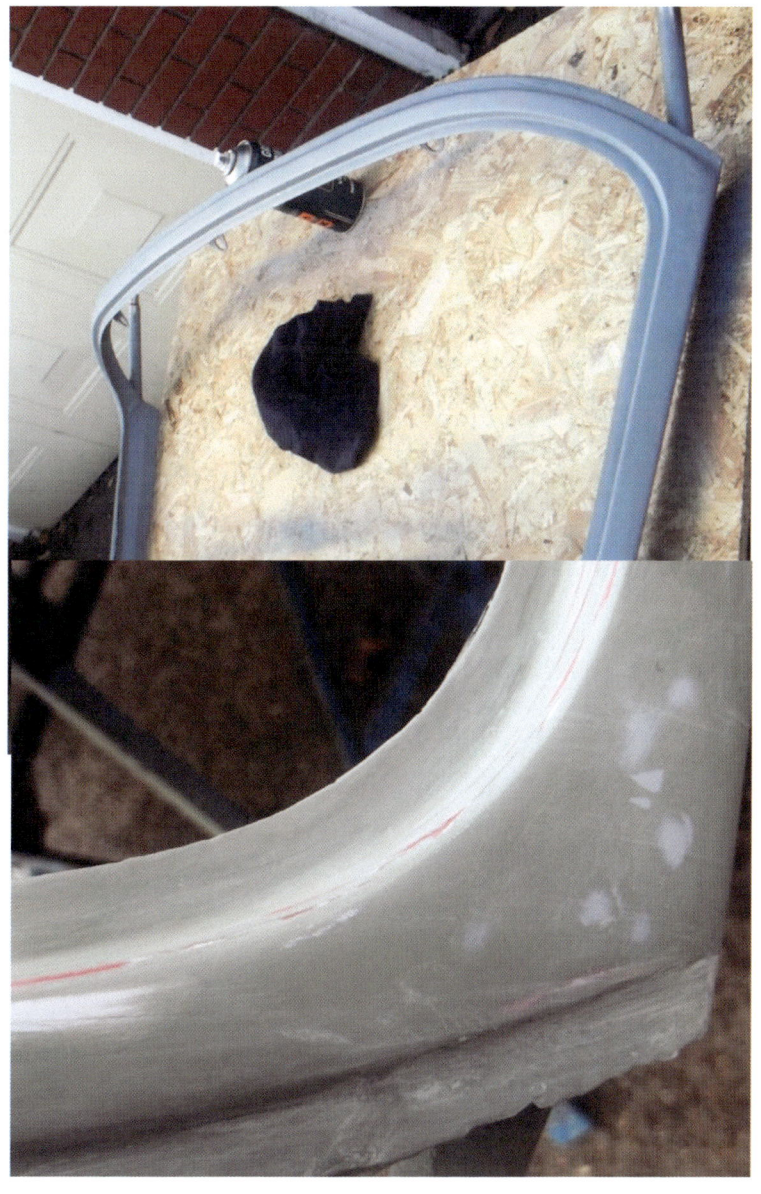

I made a "stand" for the windscreen frame by drilling two holes in the piece of board that I was using on top of my work mate bench, to accept the "legs" of the frame, this allowed me to spray all around and underneath the frame without having to move it. With the bench outside on my drive in ideal October spraying conditions I sanded the primer using 600 grit wet or dry (wet), dried it with my hot air gun, wiped it with panel wipe, then gave it an all over "dust coat" of Truck Green cellulose. After about 15 minutes I gave the frame another coat of paint and continued this process until the frame had received 5 coats, more than enough for me to sand it back and polish it to a shine, if I didn't achieve a good enough finish from the gun (this is the beauty of cellulose paint, and I would not attempt to use any other paint under the conditions that I was having to paint my frame under). I also sanded back the vent lid using 600 grade wet or dry and gave that a few coats of paint, just in case the colour match was not spot on. While waiting for each coat of paint to dry I sanded back the front scuttle, sprayed it with primer and put stopper on any imperfections.

B.J.Tip – When spraying top coat in less than warm conditions use "anti bloom" or a thinners that has a quick flash off (drying time), it costs a bit more but it dries much quicker,

giving less chance of dust contamination or a "bloom" in the finish (though this can be polished out if you experience this).

3 hours

After giving the stopper 24 hours to fully harden I sanded back the scuttle using 600 grade wet or dry (wet), then gave it three coats of primer.

1 hour

With the paint on the frame and vent lid now dry, I checked to see how close a match it was with the bonnet and I could see that it was a slightly lighter shade, this was disappointing as it meant that it was even further away (and therefore more noticeable) from the shade of green on my off side wings and door and that I would have to paint the bonnet so that it was not so noticeable, then, another rare moment, I recalled that I had purchased enough British Racing Green paint to re spray the whole car a few years ago when there were rumours that cellulose paint was to be banned! (how could I forget something like that, old age is really catching up on me!) I had a good look around my garage and found a 2.5 litre tin of BRG paint in the roof space! I opened the tin and found it to be a shade darker than the "Truck Green" paint and a far closer match to the off side wings and door! So taking advantage of the still fine October weather, I sanded back the frame and air vent using 600 wet or dry (wet), cleaned them with panel wipe and gave them a few coats of BRG.

2 hours

With the frame and air vent put carefully to one side to let the paint harden for a couple of days I turned my attention to top coating the scuttle, as I was spraying this inside my garage, I used my air fed fully enclosed face mask and a powerful extractor fan to take over spray and paint fumes out through the partially open door. Even though I used a tack rag to take away any dust

from the panel and its surrounding area and I also dampened the garage floor to keep dust to a minimum I still noticed some contamination after I had given the scuttle a dust coat of paint followed by a good coat of paint around the edges, followed by another four coats of BRG, hopefully some of this will come out when I sand and polish the panel. I used my hot air gun to warm the panel before each coat of paint as although I was spraying inside my garage conditions were far from perfect and the October air was damp.

1 hour

I gave the paint on the scuttle 24 hours to dry (not long enough really, it should be at least 48 hours and preferably a week before sanding and polishing, but as it was only a small area and I wanted the car back on the road I felt that it was worth the risk, also I didn't want to use wet or dry paper near the new rubber seal that goes between the frame and scuttle when it was all assembled) and after sanding back the scuttle and the bottom of the windscreen frame with 1200 grade wet or dry, wet I cut the paint back with T cut and luckily all the bits of dust came out without the need for harsher cutting compound. With this done I re installed the frame using the new seal, I had been told that this was "a pig" of a job to do, but using a Teflon based lubricant and my windscreen installation tools I managed the job with no problems and the new seal makes a very positive improvement when compared to the old semi perished one, especially with the new paint.

1 hour

TR6 Rear Inner Arch / GT6 Sill Repair

When a friend bought his TR6 early in 3013 he was aware that there was corrosion in the O/S rear inner wheel arch where it attaches to the rear of the sill, so before the mot was due he brought his car to me to make the repairs for him. After jacking up the car and placing it on axle stands we removed the rear wheel to access the area. After cutting all the corrosion out with cutting discs in my small hand grinder the best way to recreate the form was to make three repair patches which were painted with weld through zinc primer on the faces that would not be accessible after welding.

FIRST PATCH WELDED IN PLACE **ON TR6**

After tack welding them in place I seam welded all the edges. My friend uses his car in all weathers so he was more interested in function rather than looks and the inner arch was already under sealed so he opted to paint the repair with wax oil under seal (this can always be cleaned off at a later date if he wants a concours finish). The inside of the repair was treated to some cavity wax.

The result was a neat looking repair that will last the life of the car and can be ground down for a concours finish should he ever get the time or inclination.

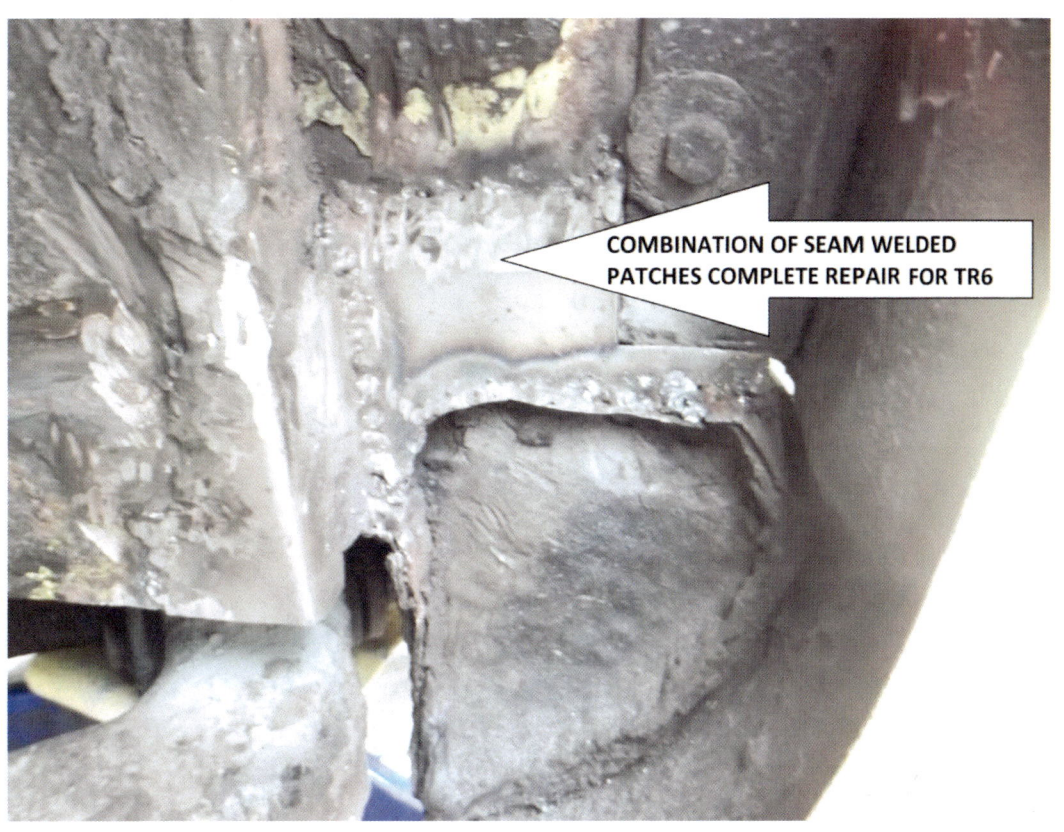

COMBINATION OF SEAM WELDED
PATCHES COMPLETE REPAIR FOR TR6

SHAPED PATCH FOR TR6

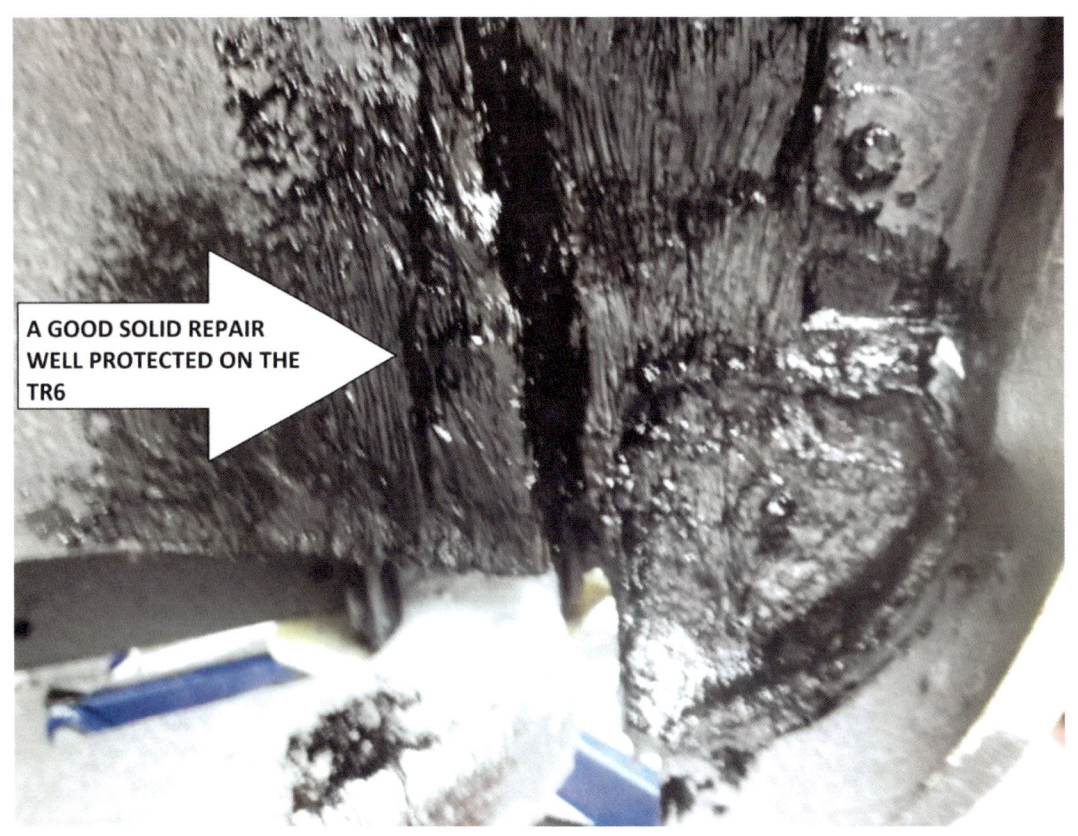

A GOOD SOLID REPAIR WELL PROTECTED ON THE TR6

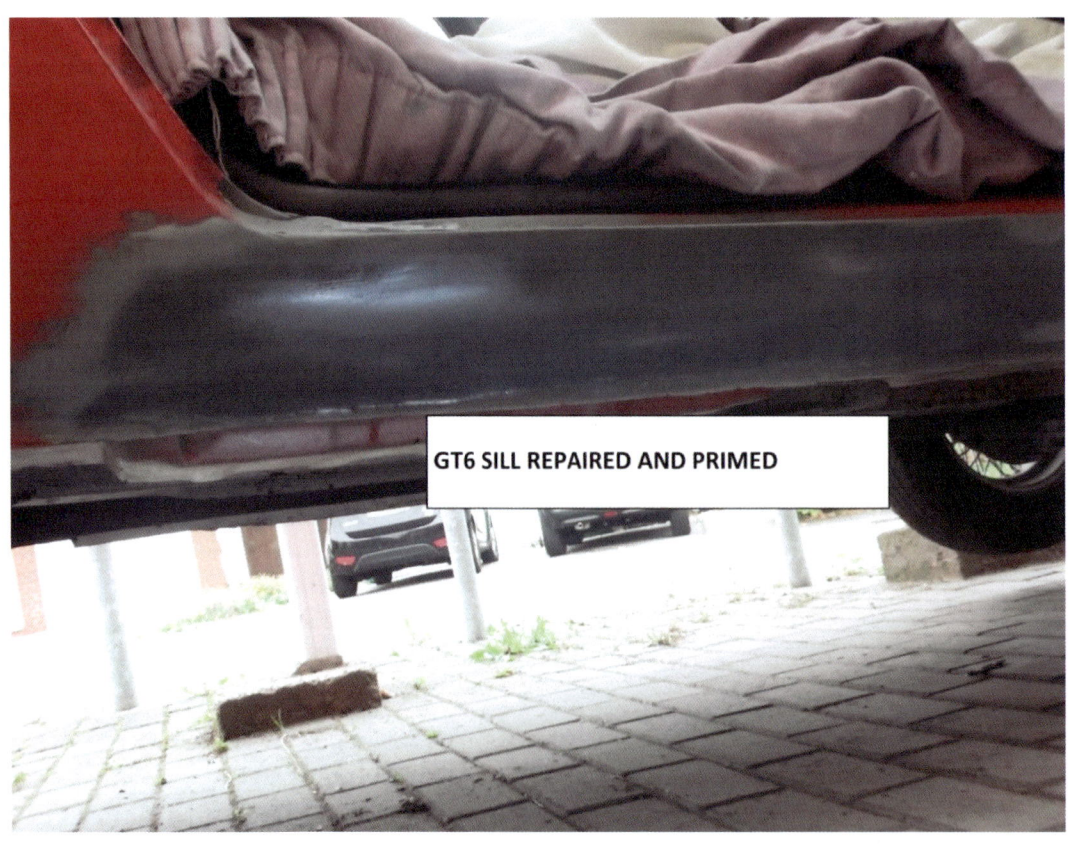

GT6 SILL REPAIRED AND PRIMED

SMALL HOLE SOON BECOMES A LARGE REPAIR WHEN CUTTING OUT RUST

Another bodywork repair that I carried out around this time was on another friend's GT6. The car had failed its mot and he was told that it needed a complete new sill. I was able to make a (large) local repair and saved him over £800, the repair was invisible after painting.

One important fact about this repair was that the original sill was kept in place and the car did not have to be braced to prevent the body from distorting with the resultant poor door gaps. The sill was also filled with cavity wax and there is no reason why this sill should ever corrode again, a massive saving for the owner.

TR4A "B" Post Repair

After putting up with the intermittent sticking when closed (I would have to give a mighty pull on the door handle) of the driver side door of my TR I finally got around to finding the fault. I checked the door latch mechanism and it looked like it was functioning correctly so I removed the anti burst catch. I opened and closed the door many times and could not get it to stick. I found a few very slight marks on the male part of the latch which indicated that I would have to adjust the two parts so that they were closer together when the door was in the closed position. This I accomplished by cutting a thin piece of rubber to use as a shim/gasket on the B post part of the latch to replace the paper gasket. I checked this out by once again opening and closing the door many times, there was no sign of the door sticking.

Now if I had addressed this issue 10 months ago when the problem started occurring this would have been the end of the story, but as I hadn't because of either pure laziness or other more important car related jobs the story continues! Please use this as a reminder of the old saying of "a stitch in time".

On very close inspection when I removed the catch from the B post I noticed a hairline crack that was running along the leading edge of the catch (not visible with the catch in position).This had obviously been caused by the poorly adjusted anti burst catch. I scrapped off all the paint along the length of the hairline fracture and cleaned it up using an emery bit in my Dremil. I then carefully welded along the length of the fracture with initially just a spot of weld every ½ inch, allowing each weld to cool then filling in the gaps, again allowing each weld to cool. Next I ground the weld flush, gave it a coat of etch primer and applied a skim of filler. I then applied waxoil underseal to the back of the B post.

The next day I used 320 graded wet or dry to sand back the filler and gave the area a coat of primer. After this dried I applied a bit more filler to the imperfections.

After leaving this for another 24 hours I sanded back the filler and primer using 320 then 600 wet or dry then gave it 3 quick coats of primer and applied some stopper.

This was then left for another 24 hours to dry after which I sanded back the stopper with 600 wet or dry then applied 3 coats of primer. The aerosol can of Fern Green arrived from the suppliers so I sanded back the primer then using my hot air gun to warm the area (as it was freezing cold) and after having stood the spray can in hot water for about half an hour I applied 5 coats of top coat. I have to say that the supplied aerosol can had an excellent spray pattern and was very easy to use, far less time consuming than setting up one of my small "detail" spray guns and mixing the paint with thinners.

I left the paint to harden fully for a week then I sanded the top coat with 1200 wet or dry then polished it up using "T" cut. Then I re fitted the anti burst catch. I have to say that the repair is invisible thanks to the "T" cut blending in any paint colour difference that there might be.

SECTION 8 Miscellaneous

High Torque Starter Motors

Something to think about or at least be aware of.

High Torque starter motors for TR's have been on sale for many years, here is an account of **my experience** with one of the ones available. I had installed this a few years ago and had been pleased with its performance, but when it developed a fault I re fitted the original standard type with the intention of repairing the High Torque starter and re installing it when repaired, however, when I removed the High Torque starter motor I noticed that there was slight damage to my flywheel's ring gear. On examination of the High Torque the starter motor a thought occurred to

me. The High Torque motor "throws" the gear forward into the flywheel ring gear to engage and turn the engine over. The standard starter motor "pulls" the gear back into the flywheel ring gear to engage and turn the engine over. The gear teeth on both High Torque and standard starter motor bendix gears have their gear teeth manufactured with a lead on them so that if they are not lined up perfectly with the flywheel gears they will still engage with the help of the leads on the flywheel ring gear and not just crash into the flywheel ring gear and cause damage.

Can you see my point? The lead on my TR4A flywheel ring gear is installed to accommodate the standard starter motor! To use the High Torque starter motor the ring gear would have to be turned around on the flywheel so that the leads on the ring gear matched the leads on the High Torque starter motor. This is the reason that there was slight damage to my ring gear, if I had continued to use the High Torque motor this damage would have become worse and maybe destroyed the ring gear.

The installation instructions that I had with the High Torque motor did not point this out and it may have been designed to engage with the non lead side of the flywheel ring gear, but on my car this has obviously not been the case as damage has occurred.

There are many Hi Torque starter motors on the market for many different cars, but if you have installed one on your Triumph I would just check that you do not have an issue before serious damage occurs.

Indicator Buzzers / Alarms

As our cars get older and more worn one of the things that often gets overlooked is the fact that the indicators can fail to self-cancel. It only has to happen once that you forget to cancel your left turn indicator and for another vehicle to pull out in front of you that the real implications of a non-self-cancelling indicator can "hit" home. About 5 years ago this happened to a friend of mine and his immaculate GT6 was all but written off. It was at that time that I decided to fit some Buzzers/Alarms to my Triumphs .

On my Toledo and Herald it was a simple task of wiring one alarm in line with the flasher unit, however, on my TR4A I had to use 2 alarms due to the flasher unit used on the car, but at only a few pounds each it didn't break the bank. The alarms do not use much current and so do not affect the flash rate nor damage the flasher units (well mine have been fitted for about 15 years and I have had no problems), but are very loud which is a bonus when driving with the soft top down and the sun reflecting off the dashboard dials, but I have regulated the volume on mine by putting some insulation tape around them a layer at a time until an acceptable volume is reached.

They have proved very useful over the years as I can't wait to turn a corner and cancel the annoying sound they make!

The Buzzers are only small and easily fit behind a dashboard either tie wrapped or tapped to the wiring loom etc. I have included an image (with a 5 pence piece to indicate physical size) so that anyone who wants to make this simple upgrade to their car and get a better "Buzz" from driving it can identify them easily from any of the well known auction sites, just type in 12v DC buzzer/alarm.

TR4A Wire Wheel Change to Minilite Replicas

Another change that I have made to my TR4A was to swap the original wire wheels to Alloy Minilite replica wheels. The TR4A came with wire wheels fitted as standard, earlier TR4s came with steel wheels as standard. There were a number of reasons why I made the change, 1) I don't like cleaning cars and wire wheels take some cleaning. 2) My wire wheels were at the end of their days with slight wear on the splines, spokes becoming loose etc, 3) There was a bargain sale of the Minilite replica wheels at a well-known TR specialist shop. I was also hoping for the added bonus of better handling with the more rigid wheels.

I bought five wheels and had new tyres fitted by a local mobile tyre fitter, he found that one wheel needed quite a few weights to balance it, so this was used as the spare. I noted that the trim board in the boot was now resting on the slightly wider wheel. When I started to fit the wheels I noted that the original wheel studs were not protruding enough to get a good enough fit on the (new) wheel nuts. I checked out part numbers from my TR4/4A parts book and found that the earlier TR4 with the steel wheels had a different part number to the TR4A which I assumed was for longer wheel studs. I called the shop from where I had bought the wheels and they confirmed that I would need to buy the TR4 wheel studs which were indeed longer (I found it disappointing that they did not inform me that I would need the longer studs when I ordered the wheels as I had told them what car they were for, it would have been possible to use the old studs and tighten up the wheel nuts, but this could have resulted in the nuts slackening off or stripping the threads as the nuts would not have been deep enough on the studs, please be aware of this if you have carried out the same conversion and haven't changed your studs), so nearly another £100 worse off and the new longer studs on order.

To fit the front wheel studs I had to remove the brake calliper and hub then slacken off the disc brake bolts and move the disc slightly away from the hub to obtain enough room to fit the new studs. With the wheels in place I took the car for a run and found that the handling in tight bends was much improved, however, when pulling up onto my drive on tight lock there was a "grinding" noise from the front of the car. I jacked the front of the car up and placed axle stands under the chassis. By turning the steering on full lock both ways I found that the top trunnion bolt heads were coming into contact with the wheel rims. To get over this I made a 1.5mm shim/spacer for each wheel out of aluminium sheet and placed them on the front hubs. I checked to see if the trunnion bolts were now clear, but they were not, so I made up another 1.5mm shim/spacer for each wheel and tried again. This time the wheels were clear of the runnion bolt heads, so I lowered the car down and took it for another run, this time there was no problem.

The Minilite replica wheels stay cleaner than the original wire ones and on the odd occasion when I do throw a bucket of soapy water over the car they come up like brand new. Perhaps one day when I can't afford the petrol to use the TR I will buy a nice set of chrome spoke wheels, but for now the Minilite replica wheels suit me down to the ground (pardon the pun).

TR 4A Oil Pressure Gauge and Valve

Over the last 12 months the oil pressure gauge in my TR4A had developed an annoying trait, the needle sticking at around 50 psi on de acceleration. This had gradually become more regular and as I was never happy with the visual quality of the oil pump that I had fitted when I rebuilt the engine (although all the tolerances were spot on) I started to worry that the gauge wasn't giving a correct oil pressure reading. When hot the gauge was indicating about 18 psi on tick over of 600 rpm (30 psi when cold) and at 3500 rpm it was indicating 70 psi.

I had amongst my spares a SMITHS gauge which I thought I would change for the original JAEGER gauge as a temporary measure to check the oil pressure while I tried to source a JAEGER item or had my original repaired and re calibrated. To do this I had to remove the speedometer, rev counter and the glove box door stay, the wooden dash board facia could then be eased forward after removing the retaining screws to give me enough room to remove the JAEGER gauge and replace it with the SMITHS gauge.

Before re fitting the other gauges and dashboard facia I started the engine and saw that the oil pressure was at 50psi (cold) at tick over and checked that the new fibre washer that I had used in the oil pressure gauge union was not leaking. All looked good so the other gauges and dashboard facia were re fitted.

On my first run with the "new" gauge in place I noted that it indicated **at least** another 5 psi at tick over when hot and right through the "rev range". Gaugetastic I thought. The next step was to try adjusting the oil pressure valve.

To do this it should be quite simple, slacken off the locknut on the top of the body that the oil filter (or adapter for a spin off type filter) screws onto and turn the adjusting screw clockwise, however, with a socket on the locking nut, the entire valve moved so I thought it best to remove the valve and give all the components a good clean.

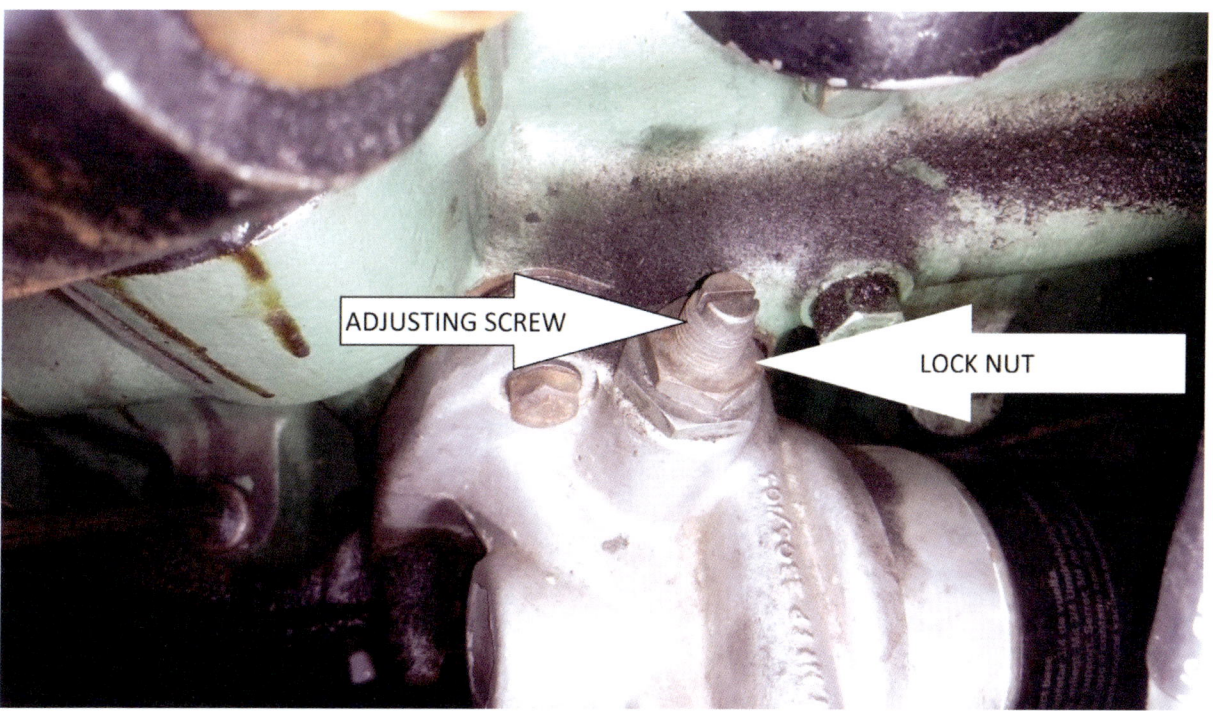

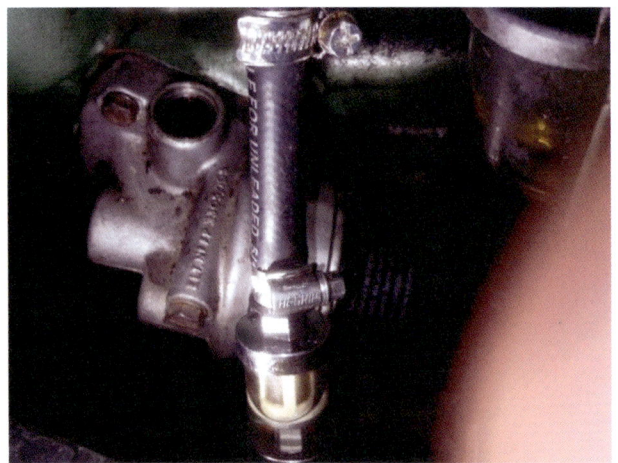

. With it removed I stripped it down and cleaned the body, spring and ball bearing but the adjusting screw was seized solid in the locking nut so I had to use a blow torch on it to free it up. With this carried out I screwed the adjusting screw clockwise about 5/8 of a turn then reassembled the valve. Then using Wellseal to seal the lock nut to the valve body and also to seal the valve body to the housing I screwed the complete valve in place.

The engine was started and the oil pressure gauge indicated 60 psi with the engine cold,

this dropped to 28 psi at 600rpm when the engine reached normal running temperature with a reading of 80 psi at 3500 rpm, Valvetastic I thought and I wouldn't want the oil pressure to be any higher or the oil would probably start leaking out of gaskets and seals.

The next run that I took the TR on was to the Shepton Mallet Show November 5th 2017, and after moving less than a mile in 20 minutes due a traffic jam caused by a road closure the engine oil could not have been any hotter or thinner. The oil pressure gauge was indicating about 30 psi at 600rpm then when the traffic started moving, 50 psi at 1500 rpm, 60 psi at 2000 rpm and 80 psi at 3500. The only action left to take was to take the oil pressure gauge out, strip it down then place the Jaeger "face" in the fitted SMITHS gauge. I did ask a gauge "specialist" at Shepton Mallet if he could repair my JAEGER gauge and he said "Yes, for £70", but how could he give me a price without even examining the gauge to see what was wrong with it, perhaps he was psychic? Hard to gauge that I thought!

Whether six cylinders or four, a TR4A is more (especially with good oil pressure)

Nitrogen in TR4A Tyres

In February of 2015 I was having a new set of front tyres fitted to my TR4A (the same make and type as the ones being replaced) when the tyre fitter suggested that I have them filled with Nitrogen instead of air, the claimed benefits were that the tyres would last longer due to the fact that Nitrogen allows your tyres to "run cooler" and that the car would handle better. I asked some obvious questions like could air be mixed with the Nitrogen if the tyres needed to be inflated and he said that they could but the benefits would be reduced. He also said that the Nitrogen would not corrode the mag alloy wheels (as compressed air does) that are fitted to my TR. The cost at the time was £2.50 per tyre so for the total cost of an extra £12.50 I decided to have all 5 tyres filled with Nitrogen.

Although I have to say that I did not notice any significant difference in performance, I would usually be looking to change the front tyres after about 8000 miles, but with 10,000 miles covered with the Nitrogen filled tyres (during this time I have not had to inflate them), the tyres still had more than a legal tread limit, also the rear tyres would have needed changing by now and they were also still well above the legal limit. So when I have the tyres replaced will I have them filled with Nitrogen? You bet!

TR Wiper Rack Refurbishment

While returning from a run to the Bristol Restoration Show (November 3rd 2013) in the pouring rain I watched enviously through my rear view mirror as my friend's TR6 windscreen wipers swept majestically across the screen wiping away the rain, he seemed to be taunting me as he flicked from first to second speed with the wiper arms reacting instantly. Enough of this I thought, I'll sort out my slow, erratic and hesitant wiper action before the next run (or at least for Le Mans in 8 months time).

If the wheel boxes had been slack on the rack causing the wiper arms to be "floppy" I could first of all tried disconnecting the rack from the motor gear box and twisting it around through 180 degrees before re fitting it, this would have turned any wear in the rack to the opposite side of the gears in the wheel boxes, then to improve things even more I could have slackened off the wheel boxes (gaining access from under the dashboard and removing the covers) and turned the shaft until an unworn section of the gear meshed with the rack, but as my issue wasn't "floppy" wiper arms a complete strip down was the best course of action.

I had had the wiper motor out a few years ago and reconditioned so I was reasonably sure that the motor and gearbox were not at fault.

The next day saw me in my garage and after checking that the motor was receiving sufficient current by connecting it directly to the battery and that making no difference I started looking at the hassle involved in accessing the various parts. I know I thought, instead of fiddling about under the dashboard I could use my plasma cutter to cut away the plenum chamber which would then give me good access, then weld the chamber back together afterwards, the only thing that stopped me from doing this was the fact that I would still have to fiddle around under the dashboard to remove the wiring and other combustible substances. Damn, I was going to have to do the job the boring way.

After disconnecting the battery I removed the glove box (longest part of the entire job was emptying the glove box and trying to fit everything back in afterwards), the speedo and rev counter, then the heater vents (I didn't gain much room on the O/S by unbolting that vent as I

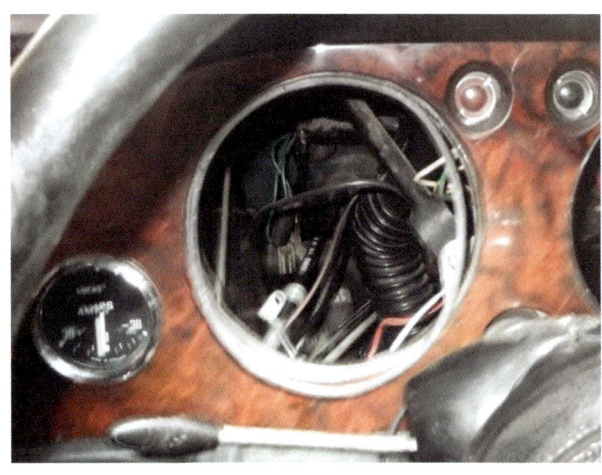 

would have had to remove more hardware to completely remove the vent from under the dashboard). Next I removed the two bolts from under the dash that secure the wiper motor. Working in the engine bay I marked the position of the domed cover in relation to the top flat cover (this dictates the wiper arm park position) and then removed the top from the motor and gear box and after removing a C clip I was able to pull the central electrical contact off the gear wheel which in turn allowed me to remove the actuating arm and then disconnect the motor from the rack. I removed the wiper arms and washer jet bushes (which I should have left in place until I had unbolted the wheel box clamping bolts). Once more under the dashboard I used a 5/16" socket (very tight fit) on the wheel box bolts that clamp the two halves in place and after removing the two bolts from both boxes I was able to remove the wheel boxes. It would helped to have someone hold the wheel boxes firmly from the top of the plenum chamber when carrying this out (as I had removed the washer jet bushes) and just as I finished this awkward task along came a friend of mine, typical!

I drew the rack out and after degreasing and cleaning the rack and wheel boxes I gave them a good examination. The gears seemed to be in excellent condition but the one wheel box was extremely tight to turn so after prising off the rubber seal from under the splined boss where the wiper arm fits I left it to soak in penetrating oil, I then repeated this with the other wheel box. Turning my attention to the rack I found evidence of wear in the areas where the wheel boxes locate so rummaging about in my spare part cache I found a rack from a 1500 Spitfire which was in far better condition (and as the TR wheel boxes would locate in a different position to the Spitfire's there would be no wear in those areas) and seemed like it would fit after being cut to length.

I gave the wheel boxes a good oiling while rotating the shafts until they were nice and free and then I stretched three O rings over each splined boss to replace the rubber seals.

With the Spitfire rack cut to length I tested to see how smooth the rack felt in the three tubes, I had to reform two very slightly to achieve a nice smooth operation. With the wheel boxes clamped in position on the rack with the tubes and all moving parts given a coat of copper grease I once more checked that everything operated smoothly. Then I dismantled the rack assembly, placed the tube that attaches to the motor and the middle section tube on the rack and fed it carefully through the aperture in the plenum chamber. Then working from inside each foot well I installed the two wheel boxes and the end tubing through the wheel box cover apertures. This was a bit

fiddly working on my own so to make it easier I loosely fitted the washer jet bushes to keep the wheel boxes in position. The motor was then re installed and the pre marked park position on the domed cover lined up with its corresponding mark. The washer jet bushes were then removed, sealant applied to their mating faces and then re installed.

With the battery re connected and the ignition on I pulled the wiper switch and all seemed good. After turning them off and allowing them to park I installed the wiper arms and gave them another try. Even with a dry windscreen there was a marked improvement.

I took the opportunity to spray some cavity wax through the wheel box covers into the plenum chamber before re fitting the covers with new sealant. The vents, glove box, speedo and rev counter were then all put back in place. When I tried the wipers they seemed to be operating extremely well.

I had been lucky with this job as I never had to buy any parts and the speed of the wipers was very much improved. Unfortunately I had to wait a while to find out how big an improvement there was actually clearing rain off the windscreen as living here in sunny Wales we weren't due get any for another seven months, but when it did rain the difference was well worth the effort.

Seat Repair

Although I carried out this repair on the seat of my Triumph 2000 Saloon, the same method and principles can be used on most models of Triumphs or other classic cars. When I bought the car it had a large hole in the right hand panel on the driver seat base which needed attending to.

For the repair I opted to choose a colour that would be a contrast to the original colour, but really I should have tried to procure a piece of vinyl that was a good match to the original seat, although I have rarely found that it is possible to do so due to discolouration of the original

material. My plan was to replace both the left and right hand side panels so that it looked "equal" then at a later date I would also change the panels in the passenger seat. I say a later date because I find upholstering seats very tedious, time consuming and boring, but I was hoping that the result would be better than having the large hole.

First of all I removed the entire seat from the car. I then carefully removed all the clips and very gently prised the cover from the foam to limit any damage that would be caused by breaking the bond of the adhesive.

The damaged panel was carefully removed and, using it as a template, I marked around it on a piece of vinyl (£3.49 for ½ a metre) but keeping a uniform ½ inch all around the area that would be visible.

Then with the seat cover turned inside out I stitched the new panel in place. I did not use a sewing machine as there were many layers in some places and I would have lost control, so this process took me three hours!

I could not face doing the other panel that day, but a load of beer in the evening gave me fresh enthusiasm for the next day so I repeated the process on the left hand panel. After this I re fitted

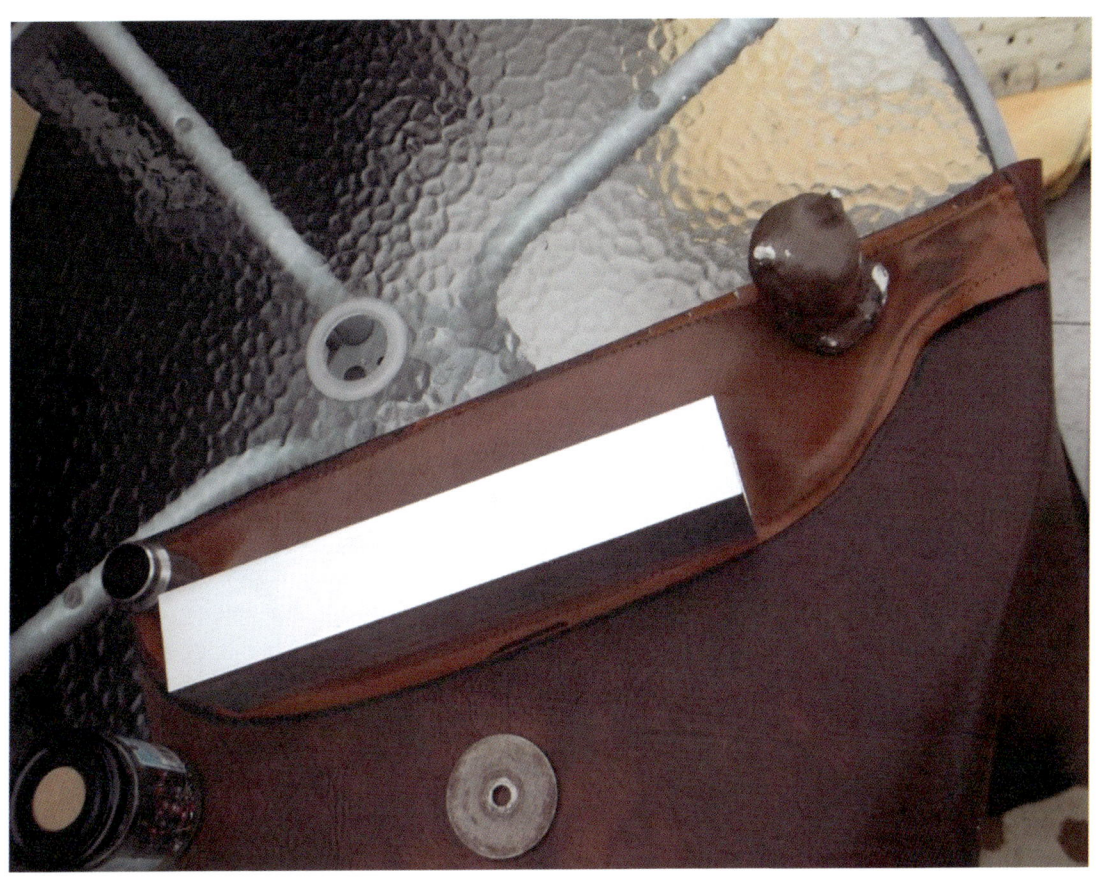

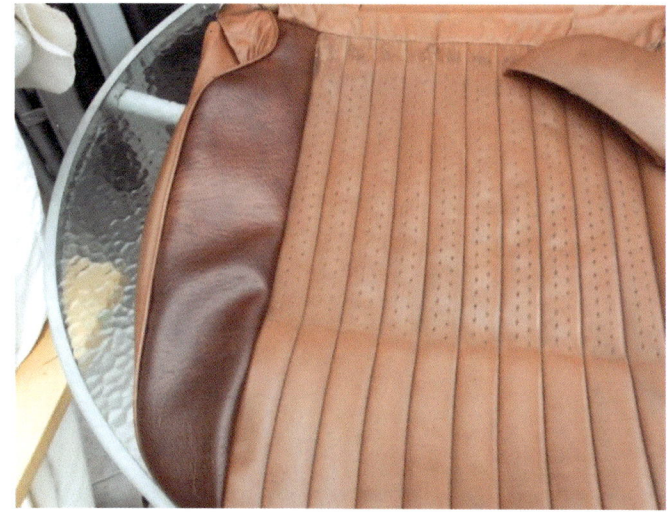

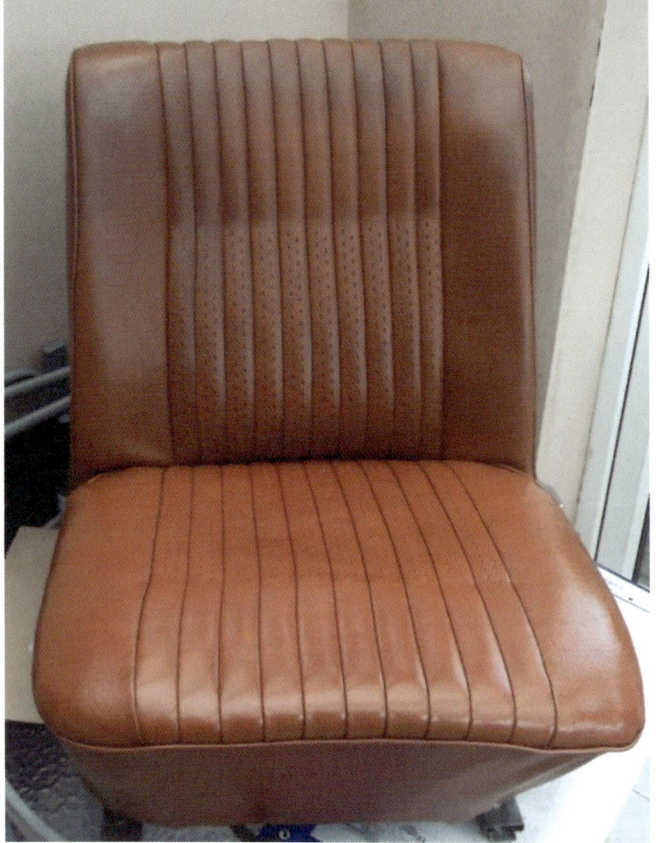

the cover to the seat base using contact adhesive and the clips. I knew that it would be many months before I could summon up the enthusiasm to remove the panels from the passenger seat and replace them with the same colour that I had used on the driver seat, so I thought that I would experiment with one of the leather/vinyl paints that are available. I ordered a spray can of tan colour and tried it on an off-cut of the material that I had bought, the match to the original colour was excellent! I left it to dry overnight and then I screwed the painted off-cut up, and stretched it this way and that way to see if the paint would crack or peel off, it didn't! I decided to mask off the whole top of the seat base and after giving it a good clean I applied two coats of the Tan paint and left it to dry.

The end result is a nice looking seat with no rips or tears, but with the base cover looking slightly different (if you look closely) in colour to the back, but this would be the same if I had been able to buy a new cover for the seat base due to discolouration over the years. So if you have a seat that badly needs a repair you can with the help of a sharp needle, rot proof thread and an off-cut of vinyl (perfect if your seats are black) plus a tube of contact adhesive make your car's interior a better place to be in, the total cost of this repair including the paint was less than £16 and it has made a huge difference to the car's interior. I just wish that I had tried the paint before renewing the second panel on this seat!

Whether 6 cylinders or 4 a TR (or 2000 Saloon) is more!

TR Reserve Bonnet Release Cable

This is an issue that can affect owners of TR4, TR4A, TR250, TR5 and TR6 cars. I know that it is quite a well known issue, but for those who own one of these models and have not heard of the potential problem, this article could save you a lot of grief in the future. If you do not have a reserve or secondary method of operating your bonnet release mechanism I would advise that you do it sooner rather than later.

For Spitfire, Herald and GT6 cars opening the bonnet is simply a matter of lifting the catches on the sides of the bonnet and lifting it up, but on the TR4 and its derivatives the bonnet (which is hinged at the front) is released by pulling a knob (which is under the dashboard) that is attached to a cable which in turn releases the latch that holds the bonnet down, with the latch released the spring then pushes the bonnet up slightly to enable you to get your fingers under the bonnet to open it.

Now this latch system is located between the central battery box and the master cylinders on TOP of the bulkhead (not the front of the bulkhead where you would be able to access it from underneath the car), so imagine the scenario you are faced with when one day you pull the release knob and the cable snaps or (as what happened to my best mate Chipmunk on his TR6) the screw that holds the cable into the locking collar on the latch works loose and the cable just pulls out! Chipmunk was lucky, he had recently totally restored his car and it only took 2 evenings with the car on a 4 poster lift and my help holding his endoscope camera while he used various bent bars to actuate the release mechanism from beneath the car (imagine having to carry this out if you did not have access to a lift or endoscope camera and were relying on axle stands to give you decent height when lying on the floor in an attempt to gain access with a lever to the mechanism that you couldn't see), if his latch had been stiff, then I doubt that he would have managed to get enough leverage on it to open it. He even consulted a well known TR forum (we both used to be members of that club) and one piece of advice was to cut a hole in his bonnet (with dimensions and position given) to enable access to the latch system! Very drastic especially as Chipmunk's bonnet was a brand new Heritage item, but no doubt, someone, somewhere had at one time had to resort to this to open their bonnet.

Anyway as they say prevention is better than cure, so after Chipmunk had encountered this issue we both decided to add a second or reserve cable. To do this on my car I drilled a hole in the latch operating arm and installed another cable fitting, I then ran a new release cable to the front of the car so that I could access it through the grille, as a further safety measure,

I also fitted both release cables with a locking collar which would prevent the cable from pulling through the fittings on the release arm should the locking bolts on those inadvertently slacken off.

A few months after this I saw an advert in a monthly Triumph publication for a clever little mechanism that would open the bonnet should the release cable fail, from memory it cost less than £20 delivered, and so I duly bought and fitted one, it is basically a lever which you attach by drilling a hole in the side of the bonnet release mechanism which is in turn operated by a small rod for which you drill a hole in the top of the bulkhead to allow it to be accessed under the dashboard, when you pull the rod it operates the lever which in turn release the bonnet latch, very simple, very clever! So now I have three systems that I can use to open my bonnet and hopefully prevent the aggravation that a failed bonnet pull cable can cause.

I hope that any TR4 – 6 owners who read this and has not heard of this issue fits at least one of the above solutions before it happens to them.

Whether three bonnet pulls or one a TR is fun!

Printed in Poland
by Amazon Fulfillment
Poland Sp. z o.o., Wrocław